TROUBLED JOURNEY

TROUBLED JOURNEY

A MISSIONARY CHILDHOOD
IN WAR-TORN CHINA

Faith Cook

THE BANNER OF TRUTH TRUST

THE BANNER OF TRUTH TRUST
3 Murrayfield Road, Edinburgh EH12 6EL, UK
P.O. Box 621, Carlisle, PA 17013, USA

*

© Faith Cook 2004

ISBN 0 85151 878 8

*

Typeset in 12 /15 pt Goudy Old Style BT at
the Banner of Truth Trust, Edinburgh.
Printed and bound in Great Britain
by Bell & Bain Ltd.,
Glasgow

TO MY SON
SIMON

AT WHOSE SUGGESTION AND
ENCOURAGEMENT THIS
ACCOUNT WAS WRITTEN

Contents

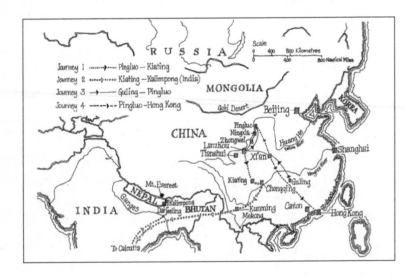

China and the surrounding region (top).
The principal journeys described (bottom).

Preface

At the repeated request of my family and friends, I have at last agreed to write an account of my childhood years – years of high adventure, unusual circumstances, deprivations and deep sorrows. It has not been an easy account to write as it touches on a number of hurtful memories. It also involves issues that have been a problem, not only to me, but to many other children of missionary parents.

Why then was it written? My first aim has been to demonstrate the faith, commitment, and courage of many missionaries, particularly during the earlier part of the last century who at great personal cost left home and family to serve God in some of the far places of the earth. With fortitude and self-denial they gave their all in order to spread the Christian gospel. However, my purpose is also to suggest that sometimes their zeal was misguided. Some of the sacrifices which they, and the missionary societies that supported them, felt they must make for Christ's sake brought unnecessary suffering to both parents and children.

Although this account is disturbing in parts, I have attempted to show through my own experiences – experiences shared by many other missionaries' children known to me – a principle to which all Christians can also testify, that of the over-arching providence of God, protecting his people in situations of gravest danger and raising up unexpected help for them in times of crisis and need.

Many today have also known circumstances in life that they may wish they could forget. Perhaps some who read these pages have found it hard to deal with resentments over situations beyond their control that have affected their lives adversely. It is my hope that through the events described here they may be better able to come to terms with such problems and be encouraged to look beneath the surface of things and discover that in spite of all, God has been at work in their lives overruling all things for his glory and their own ultimate best interest.

I wish to acknowledge the help and co-operation of my brother, Christopher, in compiling this account. In some of the events we both experienced he has been able to recall some further details which I have used to enrich the narrative. Other friends who shared the same circumstances during childhood have also added valuable memories which have been a help to me.

I am grateful to our friend Ralph Ireland for reading the manuscript through for me and especially to Lady Catherwood for her warm encouragement.

FAITH COOK
August 2004

1

IN LOVE WITH A PHOTOGRAPH

A small family sat huddled together in a Wimbledon air raid shelter. It was late September 1940 and nightly bombing raids known as the Blitz were devastating London. World War II had already witnessed alarming German advances, and in July France had capitulated, leaving Britain alone to face the German might. Those raids that had begun over London on 7 September would leave more than 30,000 dead before they ended in May 1941.

Stanley and Norah Rowe, members of the China Inland Mission, had been in Christian service in China for the past eight years, but now, with their two young children, they were far from their sphere of vocation. Instead of their mission station in a small town bordering on the Gobi Desert far to the north of China, they were to be found in an underground bunker in bomb-stricken England seeking protection from yet another aerial bombardment.

'There's anuvver one, Faiff,' announced the small boy gleefully, as the wailing note of the siren died away, and the distant thud of a falling bomb reverberated through the shelter. Not quite three years of age, I was terrified and Christopher knew it. Each echoing boom intensified my fear, and

Christopher mischievously exploited my misery with calm enjoyment.

Christopher and Faith in Wimbledon, aged 5 and 3

But what circumstances had brought our family from China to England at such a time of insecurity and risk? It had all begun six years earlier when my father had fallen in love with a photograph. Born in 1904, Stanley, resolute, single-minded, and as yet unmarried, had sailed for China in 1931 under the auspices of the China Inland Mission. Founded in 1865 as a result of the vision and compassion of James Hudson Taylor, the Mission existed, as its name implied, to push forward the frontiers of the Church of Jesus Christ into the vast and largely unevangelized regions of inland China. The story of the mission had been one of heroic endurance, of intense suffering and, despite all set-backs, of steady advance. In 1929 the General Director of the Mission had issued an appeal for 200 more candidates to volunteer for service in the next two years to take up the challenge of new areas which were opening up for Christian missions. A total of two hundred and three enlisted and Stanley, who came from a long-established Methodist background, was among them.

So urgent was the need for new workers that Stanley was scarcely given any time to grasp even the rudiments of Mandarin Chinese, with all its complex tonal inflexions, before being posted to the far north-west of China. There in the provincial city of Ningxia[1] (Ningshia) – the north-westernmost point of the Mission's activities at that period – he would attempt to master the language, learning as he mixed with the people. The province of Ningxia itself, one of China's smallest, is sandwiched between the great pan-shaped province of Gansu (Kansu) to the west and Shanxi (Shensi) on the east. Much of it is arid and mountainous with, at that time, a population of only one-and-a-half million. To the west lies the high range of the Ho-Lan mountains, between six and nine thousand feet above sea level in parts, while the Yin mountain range of Inner Mongolia forms a natural northern boundary.

On the west of the province flows the wide and dangerous Yellow River, or *Huang Ho* in Chinese, so named because of its yellow waters heavy with loess sediment. The river rises high up in the Tibetan mountains, and loops its way through northern China for three thousand miles until it deposits its heavy alluvium into the waters of the Yellow Sea on China's

---

[1] The Wade-Giles spelling of place names, in use when these events took place, is given in brackets after the first use of the name. The Pinyin spelling is now in common use.

north-eastern coast. Known also as *China's Sorrow* because of its destructive flooding, its treacherous waters are broad and slow-moving at this point, flowing northward through Ningxia, enriching the surrounding countryside. In a country where spirit-worship had long held the people in bondage, there had once been an annual rite of throwing a young woman into its depths, in the hope of appeasing the river god and protecting homes and crops.

Like many of China's cities, towns, and even villages, the city of Ningxia was protected by surrounding walls. Local warlords and bandits had long roamed the area, making such protection a necessity. The wide streets in the centre gradually gave way to the mud yards and dreary grey hovels of the suburbs, typical of many Chinese towns of the time. The Hui people or Chinese Muslims formed about one third of the population. Among this community that clung resolutely to the tenets of Islam, Stanley faced a major challenge of his missionary calling. Buddhism and animism – the worship of spirits – were the major religions of the rest of the population. To these men and women, sunk in degrading rituals and tormented by fear of the vengeance of evil spirits, the young missionary would bring a message of hope through the preaching of the Christian gospel.

The days were turbulent and dangerous and in many areas law and order had completely broken down. China's central administration under General Chiang Kai-shek and his Nationalist government was ineffectual and weak. As a result local power-seekers, aided by hungry and destitute men, roamed the countryside trying to capture towns and set up regional dynasties. Ningxia came under heavy bombardment when Suen Tien Ying and his indisciplined hordes turned up at the gates of the town and started shelling, demanding admission. Meeting determined resistance he finally gave up, only to try elsewhere. Soon after this Stanley, and fellow missionary Greg Walker, were posted forty miles further north to the yet more vulnerable town of Pingluo (Pinglo) – another walled and tightly knit community. Here they would learn the language over the next two years as they worked together, preaching, teaching, and helping the people.

Meanwhile, in October 1932, the P & O liner *Corfu* steamed up the fetid Huangpo River, with its dirty waters strewn with flotsam and jetsam, on its way into Huangpo harbour, outlet for the sprawling city of Shanghai, China's most crowded conurbation. Among the passengers aboard the *Corfu* were eight young women volunteers, come to join the ever-expanding missionary personnel of the China Inland Mission. Each had consecrated desires to bring the message of the Christian gospel to China's teeming and needy population. Norah Giles was among the missionary candidates. A strong personality, she was attractive, witty and outgoing. Norah was born in 1907. She had spent much of her early childhood in India where her father had served as a captain in the Indian army. After completing her education at an English boarding school, Norah had undertaken secretarial training. She was converted at the age of twenty under the preaching of the Rev. George Campbell Morgan, then on a summer visit from America to Westminster Chapel, London. Norah later became a member of the Chapel. At that time the call to missionary service was constantly emphasized in Christian circles and, during the late 1920s, Norah had responded. It would be a life of sacrifice, a life of placing the concerns of her missionary calling before any personal consideration, with probably few opportunities ever to revisit her homeland or her parents.

This Norah knew well and accepted. So with the prayers and support of her own parents and of the members of the Chapel, she had applied to the China Inland Mission for missionary service in China.

From the deck of the *Corfu*, Norah gazed in bewilderment at the flotilla of junks, sampans and houseboats bobbing cheekily up and down among the stately ocean-going vessels – her first sight of Chinese life. Slowly the passengers disembarked and were soon faced with an army of rickshaws, each owner eager for the work of carrying the arrivals to their destinations. For Norah and her friends this would be to the Mission's headquarters at 1531, Sinza Road, two multi-storied buildings in one of Shanghai's busy streets.

Norah had never seen a rickshaw before; she climbed in gingerly, wondering if it would be safe, and was amazed at the speed with which its owner set off, pulling his two-wheeled carriage deftly along the crowded dusty streets. A city of contrasts, Shanghai had two distinct faces and Norah saw both as she passed: The one half-westernized, with its bustle and commerce, and the other of desperate poverty. Emaciated men and women looked old and haggard, and even little children lay in the streets, many half-starved, some clearly dying.

Unlike Stanley, Norah was given opportunity during her first six months in China to learn Mandarin at the mission's language school. Situated in Yangzhou, one time home of the Venetian traveller, Marco Polo, the school presented an intensive course of study using the skills of Chinese tutors who came in each day to give individual as well as group instruction. Here she mingled with new missionaries from America, Germany, Switzerland, Norway, Sweden and other parts, many struggling with homesickness as they tried to acclimatize to a new culture. A daunting language, Chinese has at least 1,200 characters, many subdivided into four distinctive tones. Norah found the course arduous and though at times she felt like giving up, she gradually began to master the intricacies of this new language.

Soon Norah would be allocated to a permanent sphere of service, but before that happened she was offered a time of relaxation in a hill resort in the province of Honan in Central China. It was delightfully cool after the intense heat of Yangzhou, and a welcome respite following the exhausting study of recent months. Before long Norah was designated to a small town also in Honan province where she would work alongside more senior missionaries. But one day she had an unexpected visitor. A young missionary whom she had never met before had arrived. Stanley Rowe, tall, bespectacled, with wavy black hair, but looking travelled-stained and far from well, had come from distant Ningxia and seemed anxious to speak to Norah.

Stanley had been seriously ill – so ill, in fact, that at one point his life had hung in the balance. Suffering from a severe bout of typhus fever, common in a land where rats, fleas and mosquitoes, and the diseases they carried, were endemic, he had been cared for by a young missionary nurse, Wendy Maxwell, one of that same group who had sailed to China with Norah. After her language study course, Wendy had been stationed in Ningxia. One of her assignments, in addition to her missionary work, was the care of sick missionaries in the area. Stanley was among her first patients.

Under Wendy's skilful nursing Stanley had gradually rallied, but not surprisingly, as he faced the long slow climb back to health, the sick man had become deeply depressed. In order to raise his spirits his well-meaning nurse, who was already engaged to marry Stanley's fellow worker, Greg Walker, had decided to show her patient a photograph of a young friend of hers who had sailed to China with her. Looking at Norah Giles' attractive features, the sick man was clearly impressed. 'She's lovely,' he remarked, 'I think I will marry her.'

As soon as he was well enough, Stanley decided on a long journey across China to the Honan town, having learned that the young woman in the photograph was working there.

Regardless of the advice or misgivings expressed by his area supervisor of the missionary society, Stanley prepared to set off. As might be expected, Norah was astonished by the arrival of her visitor and even more so when he did not hesitate to make his intentions clear. The ardour of her surprising suitor swept

Norah off her feet and it was not long before she yielded to Stanley's advances. And marry him she did – to the dismay of her father in England, who felt that such a method of courtship was highly irregular. 'Just walk in, as it were, with a few preliminaries . . .', was his cryptic comment to his would-be son-in-law. Women missionaries were not expected to marry until they could read at least one of the Gospels in colloquial Chinese. Norah had not found the language easy, but before long she had fulfilled this minimum condition and the wedding was fixed to take place in Honan in April 1935. Even in such unlikely circumstances, it assumed all the features of a stylish English wedding. Stanley was dressed in a smart double-breasted suit with pinstripe trousers! Norah, like all brides on their wedding day, looking a picture of serene beauty, with her flowing white dress, satin shoes and long veil, complete with bouquet of tulips and carnations.

Then came the long journey north as Norah accompanied Stanley to his distant mission station in Pingluo. Greg Walker had already left to be married to Wendy, the young nurse who had cared for Stanley, so missionary work in that far-flung corner of China had been in temporary abeyance. On the way back to Pingluo, not far from Lanzhou (Lanchow), capital city of Gansu province, the newly-weds had to navigate a part of the Huang Ho River, known for its treacherous rapids. Journeying north to Ningxia, the quickest way was to travel down river by raft – a flimsy vessel created by tying together inflated sheep skins covered over with planks of wood.

It was a risky mode of travel and no match for the mighty Huang Ho when it was in one of its most fickle moods. Tales of tragedies in that part of the river were common folklore among the people. Soon Stanley and Norah's makeshift craft was caught in swirling rapids. Try as he might the boatman could not control his raft. As it eddied in helpless circles in the current, it became clear that the only hope of saving their lives was to lighten the cargo by tipping goods overboard. The missionaries had few personal possessions apart from a small metal bathtub packed with all their wedding presents. To throw all these gifts, so recently and sacrificially donated by their friends, into the turbulent waters seemed a desperate expedient. The struggle for Stanley was intense, for he was one of life's natural hoarders. As the young couple well knew, only a few years earlier a member of their own mission had been drowned in similar circumstances. So now they realized they had little choice. The metal bathtub had to go – and gradually all their household goods sank from sight. Some days later the tub itself floated to shore empty: an ironic reminder of their loss. Hard as it was, such was the cost of missionary service.

When at last they reached their distant mission station, Norah, whose previous way of life little prepared her for the hardships she must experience in north-west China, found much to sadden, surprise and even to annoy her as they began life together in that distant outpost of civilisation. She was horrified to see the women hobbling along on tiny bound feet. Baby girls had their toes bent inwards and bound down soon after birth, for men, so they said, liked small feet in their women folk, with little regard as to whether or not they could walk on such deformed, clubbed feet. The law prohibiting the custom in 1911 had scarcely filtered through to this remote area, and small children were still subjected to this mutilation, while many older women died prematurely because they could scarcely walk, let alone earn their living. Nor was there any privacy for the white woman. Wherever

In Love with a Photograph

Norah turned the crowds gathered to stare at her, many pointing in disgust at her 'large' feet. Used to the variety of colours of Western clothes, Norah discovered that the entire population, here as well as in other parts of China, appeared to be dressed in dark blue – the better-placed men in full-length padded gowns, and the women in short jackets and trousers gathered tightly at the ankle.

The weather in that area of China varied from blistering heat in summer to winter temperatures that could plunge to a merciless minus 40°C. Added to this, bitter winds from across the Gobi Desert would pierce through the padded gowns worn by missionaries and locals alike. These circumstances made life difficult for the newly-married couple and particularly for Norah, unused to primitive living conditions, rat-ridden accommodation, and hostile weather. The problems were the more acute because she was already pregnant with her first child.

The presence of a visiting missionary doctor in Ningxia at the very time that Norah's baby was due was a welcome provision for the young mother. She travelled there shortly before Christmas, soon joined by Stanley, remaining until after the birth of their son, Christopher, early in February 1936. Only twenty months later Norah and Stanley's second child was due, but this time there was no medical help near at hand, and the expectant mother had to endure a far longer and jarring ride mainly by cart to the hospital at Lanzhou. Travel was by mule cart, for no railway yet linked Lanzhou with other Chinese cities. The journey of more than 350 miles to the mission hospital seemed endless as the cart jogged erratically along the bumpy tracks, and Norah and Stanley struggled to keep their lively eighteen-month-old son amused.

Lanzhou, the provincial capital of Gansu, was not yet the polluted industrial city it has now become, but the choking dust storms would sweep in from the desert, smothering every object with thick yellow loess dust and reducing visibility to a bare minimum. A gateway to the vast province of Qinghai to the west, Lanzhou stood on the travel route from Beijing through the Gobi Desert into Mongolia. The city itself was situated on one bank of the Huang Ho, while the hospital was built on a hill overlooking the river on the other. Arching across the restless waters between was the recently built Iron Bridge, constructed by Belgian engineers after the discovery of oil in the area; beyond lay the Blue Lotus Hills. The hospital, called the Borden Memorial Hospital, was erected in 1913 from funds left by William Borden of Yale, a young millionaire who died before he could accomplish his desire to reach China's Muslims with the Christian message. Staffed by dedicated missionary doctors and nurses, the hospital provided a central point in the province of Gansu, not only for the medical needs of the people, but also as a point of contact with the impoverished millions who lived along the shores of that mighty river and far beyond.

Arriving safely at last, Norah and Stanley eagerly awaited the birth of their second child. Both had hoped for a daughter, so when I was born at the end of October 1937, they were highly pleased. They decided to give their baby a Chinese name as well as her English one, and looking with hopeful eyes at the small newly-born bundle, called me *Shou-Ming*, which means 'bright and beautiful'. Despite dangerously low temperatures, the family set off six weeks later for Ningxia once more. It would have been wiser to wait for better weather conditions but Stanley, for whom his missionary labours remained his overriding concern in life,

Journey by mule cart in north-west China

insisted on the journey even though it subjected his two small children to serious risk.

Across rough and icy mountain tracks the small party bumped and slid as the mule-drawn cart struggled along. Sometimes the path wound alarmingly near the edge of sheer precipitous chasms; sometimes the animals slithered and slipped as they dragged the cart along ice-filled ruts; sometimes the mules refused to budge at all. A hot water bottle kept the baby as warm as possible, but twenty-one-month-old Christopher was dangerously exposed to the biting temperatures. On occasions the only means of generating a little heat for the six-week-old baby was to stop by the roadside, gather a few sticks, light a fire and heat enough water to refill the baby's hot water bottle.

Not surprisingly, Norah also suffered from such circumstances; shortly after arriving back in Ningxia she became seriously ill with typhus fever. With the mother unable to nurse her child and no powdered baby milk or feeding bottles available, fellow missionaries spoon-fed the ever-hungry infant with watered down evaporated milk – a mixture which apparently did me no harm at all.

When Norah at last recovered, the family returned to Pingluo. Meanwhile Stanley too was facing a serious problem. His eyesight had been deteriorating badly and for no clear cause. Without medical assistance it would seem that the young missionary would soon go blind. As little help was available in that remote outpost of north-west China, the China Inland Mission decided that the best expedient was to send the family home to England in the hope that suitable treatment could be found to avert the impending disaster.

These were the circumstances that had led up to that scene in the Wimbledon bomb shelter – among my early childhood memories. The outlook for our small family was bleak. My mother, still exhausted from her recent illness, was struggling to care for us in the home of her none-too-sympathetic in-laws in Wimbledon, and my father's eyesight problems left the whole family's future in doubt. Then came a breakthrough. In the course of a regular dental check-up it was discovered that Stanley had an abscess under one tooth. That seemed a common enough occurrence, and the offending tooth was duly extracted and the abscess drained. Shortly afterwards he noticed an improvement in his eyesight. Still he made no connection between the dentistry and his sight. But gradually, as his vision grew steadily better, he came to realize that it was poison from the abscess that had been destroying his sight. Full of thankfulness to God for this remarkable improvement, Stanley applied to his missionary society for permission to return to China.

To Stanley's dismay, the mission leaders were reluctant to receive him back again. Possibly his strong-minded insistence on following a course of action that he felt to be right regardless of advice was a factor behind such objections. Nevertheless, Stanley's dedication to his missionary calling gave him a persistence that would not be denied. Again, and yet again, he applied to be reinstated, insisting that his eyes were steadily improving. Still he was not accepted.

Trained as a banker, Stanley decided to take up banking once more in a final attempt to convince the Mission leaders that his sight would be adequate for the challenges of overseas life. Complete with heavy-lensed glasses, he now spent his days poring over sheets of figures in the gloomy lighting of a Wimbledon bank. If this did not achieve his object, he reasoned, then nothing would. And at last the Director of the mission agreed that Stanley and Norah Rowe should return to China as soon as war conditions made travel feasible.

2

A MISSIONARY CALL:
A HIGH PRICE TO PAY

Determined as ever to secure the ends he had in view regardless of difficulties, Stanley booked a passage on a merchant vessel about to venture into the dangerous waters of the Atlantic. The German occupation of the French ports put all shipping sailing past the west coast of France in imminent danger, so that such an attempt was fraught with peril. With British shipping at the mercy of German U-boats, it was a highly risky decision, and one that endangered the lives of his family.

Despite the fact that the Battle of the Atlantic was raging and would soon be at its height, with 700,000 tons of British shipping lost in the month of April alone, the family set sail early in 1941 to return to China. In the protecting mercy of God, the vessel crossed the danger zone without incident. Rumour had it, however, that a torpedo, intended to destroy the merchant ship in which the family was travelling, struck a children's hospital ship instead, with the tragic loss of all on board.

Stanley and Norah knew that their return to the far north-west of China in the late spring of 1941 would not place them beyond the uncertainties and fear of war. Conflict with Japan, intermittent since 1931, had broken out in earnest on 7 July 1937. Beijing had been the first to fall and, following this conquest, the triumphant Japanese forces, numbering two million men under arms, swept down the eastern seaboard of China, pillaging Shanghai in December of that year and Nanjing (Nanking), Chiang Kai-shek's provincial capital, soon afterwards. Among the atrocities of the twentieth century, the Rape of Nanjing, as it became known, ranks high on the list. During the last weeks of December 1937 it is estimated that between 100,000 and 300,000 people were summarily executed; countless women and girls raped; the city reduced to rubble. City after city fell into Japanese hands and with their fall further alarming cruelties were perpetrated on the Chinese people.

Nor was this the only conflict in progress. Civil war in varying degrees of intensity had been on-going between the Nationalist forces under Chiang Kai-shek and the expanding Communist Party, founded in 1921. The Party had been steadily strengthening its following as the people witnessed the corruption and ineffectiveness of the Nationalist government. At last, with Japan's ever-increasing domination, the Communists and the Nationalists formed an uneasy truce and agreed to join forces against a common enemy. But even so, they could do little to arrest the Japanese advance.

Refugees from Occupied China, estimated to be some fifty million, trundled their few possessions along in carts or on their backs and swarmed into Free China from the eastern provinces. Columns of desperate men and women were strafed from the air by Japanese aircraft. Many were diseased and dying of hunger as they trudged the weary miles to the west. Their journey was made yet more hazardous by the fact that bridges had been blown up, leaving rivers only crossable using makeshift rafts. Train lines, too, had been bombed, and in 1938 the banks of the Huang Ho were deliberately breached by order of Chiang Kai-shek, anxious to prevent further Japanese incursions. The river soon transformed itself into vast artificial lakes, sometimes twenty miles in width, which swallowed up villages and roads and left millions homeless. Over 900,000 drowned or starved as a direct result of this expedient. Nine years would pass before the Huang Ho could be tamed once more and confined within its rightful bounds.

As Stanley and Norah returned to their mission station with Christopher and me they discovered the populations of towns such as Ningxia and Lanzhou swollen with refugees as those who had survived the trek sought a haven there. The outbreak of war in Europe in 1939 had given the Japanese forces yet more incentive to expand their ever-growing empire by enlarging their sphere of operations and seeking to become the dominant power in the Pacific. U.S. bases and British-owned territory, therefore, became a target of attack, with missionaries and other U.S. and British nationals in China regarded with suspicion as potential enemy personnel.

Missionaries had incessant calls upon their strength and compassion at such a time of emergency and distress. Norah soon found that the situation was fraught with other problems as well. Strictest economies had to be observed because inflation had soared to such an extent that the money sent to them by the mission for each quarter was almost worthless by the time it arrived. The missionaries must now use any remaining liberty to teach the people and to strengthen the local churches, in case all were soon compelled to withdraw and leave the country.

The China Inland Mission had a policy of moving its workers on from town to town for maximum use of opportunities open to them and as particular needs arose. Early in 1942 Stanley and Norah were asked to join those already working in Zhongwei (Chungwei), some sixty miles south of Ningxia, a longer established mission station. Christopher and I were the only children in the complex, and therefore we had none but each other and our Chinese friends as companions. Soon we became totally bilingual, our command of Chinese more accurate than that of our parents who often struggled with the confusing inflexions of the Mandarin dialect.

My own situation was about to change once more, for Christopher had turned six in February of that year and would soon be leaving home to begin his education at the mission's boarding school. The policy of sending their young children to boarding schools was rarely questioned among the missionaries, many of whom came from English middle class families and had attended such schools themselves, in line with prevailing social custom in that stratum of society. Both Stanley and Norah had attended boarding schools as children.

In addition, Hudson Taylor, heroic pioneer and policy maker of much missionary work in China, had established the regulation that the wives of missionaries should also be missionaries in their own right, able to testify to a personal call from God, and be fully engaged alongside their husbands in the work. Expressing this principle in a letter to a fellow-worker, he wrote: 'Might we not with advantage say to our candidates, "Unless you intend your wife to be a true missionary, not merely a wife, home-maker and friend, do not join us"?'[1] Such a policy meant that the married women were

[1] Dr and Mrs Howard Taylor, *Hudson Taylor and the China Inland Mission, The Growth of a Work of God*, Morgan & Scott, 1919, p. 156.

expected to give their time principally to their missionary endeavour, and would therefore find little or no opportunity to provide for the educational needs of their children. Hudson Taylor and his second wife, Jennie, had themselves set a precedent in this area. Although Jennie had to be persuaded against her own better judgement, and at much personal cost, she and her husband had left their dependent family of seven children in the care of others in England, while they returned to China to engage in missionary service.

The thinking behind such decisions and ordering of priorities was based on a widely-held literal interpretation of such Scriptures as Matthew 10:37. Here the Lord warns his followers of the danger of loving wife, husband or children more than himself – a verse understood to mean that family duties and needs should not be allowed to take precedence over the call to evangelism. Taken in isolation from other biblical teaching on the responsibilities of family life, these words were used as a rationale for the long separations between children and their parents, not only on mission fields, but also in Christian work in the home countries.

The China Inland Mission had therefore set up its own school in the attractive north-eastern coastal town of Yangtai (Chefoo) for the children of its missionaries. Staffed with gifted teachers and providing efficient medical care, it was a commendable institution that had first opened in 1881. Land had originally been purchased a year or two earlier to provide a rest centre for the missionaries as the need arose. Hudson Taylor himself, with the help of his fellow missionaries, had built the original home. This became the first of a number of buildings that made up the Chefoo School complex.

However, as World War II became more intense and widespread, this location had proved highly vulnerable to attack from Japan. Following the onslaught on Pearl Harbour in December 1941, the Japanese, in increasingly aggressive mood, rounded up both missionary staff and children of the school in Chefoo, placing them all in overcrowded boarding houses. Shortly afterwards the buildings were requisitioned for Japanese military use, and in September 1943 staff and children were removed to a civilian internment camp in Weihsien, a hundred and fifty miles south of their school. Here they would remain for the duration of the war.

There was, therefore, no alternative to setting up another school in a safer area of China, and recruiting a make-shift staff to run it. Choosing a town as far removed as possible from Japanese attack, the mission had established a school in Kiating (now called Leshan) in the western province of Sichuan (Szechwang), a province that shared a border with Tibet. This was the school to which Stanley set off in the late summer of 1942, taking six-year-old Christopher with him. Over eight hundred miles across wild and dangerous terrain lay ahead. It was a sorrowful journey for, although the child would not have realized it, any hope of seeing his home again, at least for several years, was remote. It was with a heavy heart that Stanley returned alone to his mission station.

In September 1942 Stanley and Norah were anticipating the birth of their third child. Earlier in the year they had moved yet again to establish a further mission station, this time to Dingxi (Jingji), a small town about sixty miles south-west of Lanzhou, bustling with life, noisy and crowded. Instead of the pregnant mother travelling to the Lanzhou hospital once more, a nurse, recently arrived in China, was sent down from the hospital to Dingxi to help with the delivery and, hopefully, to gain valuable practice in her language study. In mid-September a second son,

Godfrey, was added to the family. With shiny dark eyes and a cheerful disposition, the baby flourished, and soon became the centre of attention, particularly among my young Chinese friends.

However, the missionary nurse found that she had little time for language study. Soon after Godfrey's birth, Norah became seriously ill once more, this time with general septicaemia. One of the hospital doctors from Lanzhou hastily made the journey to Dingxi; long anxious weeks followed as Norah slowly recovered. With my mother ill, my father's days fully occupied with his missionary activity and my brother away at school, I was left to find my own amuse-ment much of the time. As soon as my mother was well enough our family returned to Zhongwei once more.

Infectious diseases were rife among the local children and with little medical aid available it was not surprising that the missionaries' children also succumbed to serious illness. I had developed whooping cough earlier in 1943, but when Godfrey, now eight months old, caught the infection my parents were very troubled. Would the baby pull through? Local children were dying in the epidemic and no immunization programmes had been available in the area. Day by day Norah watched helplessly as her baby lost more and more weight. Gone were the smiles with which he had delighted all who saw him. Still weak from her own serious illness, she tried to nurse Godfrey after each distressing bout of coughing, but it seemed a losing battle. At ten months old Godfrey had returned to his birth weight. Then his condition appeared to stabilize. He had weathered the storm.

Apprehensively Norah wheeled the baby out on to the verandah of the open courtyard so that the child could benefit from the rays of the late August sun. The sight of the

English baby, always a major attraction to the Chinese children, drew a number of my friends together, all crowding around the pram. Dysentery! The thought flashed through my mother's mind. She had heard that some of the local children had been ill with the condition. If Godfrey should contract the infection in his weakened state, she knew that it could easily spell the end of his short life.

Only a few days later Norah and Stanley's worst fears were confirmed. Godfrey, not quite twelve months old, sickened with dysentery. For seven days the baby struggled against the illness. No one had time to pay much attention to me but one night as I lay in bed I heard the sound of footsteps hurrying to and fro. I sensed the crisis. My father had rushed off for medical help. A doctor came and went. I half-guessed that my baby brother could not have long to live. Then I saw my father's form in the doorway, his face drawn and sad. He beckoned to me to come and take a last look at Godfrey's face.

I can never forget what I saw that night. A lovely smile lingered on the dead baby's features. What had that sick child seen in dying, so beautiful that it brought such a smile to his face? For the first time in my five years I found myself thinking of a place of light and beauty beyond the sorrows and uncertainties of this life. Many years later I understood. Surely Godfrey had smiled because the One who first said, 'Let the little children come to me', had stooped to gather yet another little one into his arms.

The local Chinese proved deeply superstitious in the face of death, and particularly the death of a white child. No one would help the stricken parents with the funeral arrangements. I saw my father knocking together a little box to act as a coffin, and then digging, until at last he had dug a hole deep enough for the small grave. I stood and watched as my young brother's body was committed to the ground – and yet not without hope of a brighter day. The words that were sung by the few that gathered there have always remained in my mind:

Around the throne of God in heaven,
Thousands of children stand,
Children whose sins are all forgiven,
A holy, happy band.

That evening as the September sun sank low in the west my mother stood forlornly near the spot where she had seen her third child buried. Then Norah noticed that the low rays of the sun had lit up the fine threads of a cobweb. Words of a hymn she knew and loved sprang to her mind:

With mercy and with judgement
My web of time he wove;
And aye the dews of sorrow
Were lustred with his love.
I'll bless the hand that guided,
I'll bless the heart that planned,
When throned where glory dwelleth
In Emmanuel's land.

3

LIFE AND WORK ON
A MISSION STATION

With Godfrey's death, and Christopher away at school, Stanley and Norah had now only one five-year-old child left with them. As always, Stanley, and to a lesser extent Norah, busied themselves tirelessly in the work of evangelism among the Chinese. Their dedication to their calling could never be doubted. I would watch as day after day my father gathered together his roll of Bible posters or his flannelgraph board and took his stand on some street corner. As he set up his equipment a small crowd would gather, mainly out of curiosity, for the Chinese had an insatiable interest in any unusual sight.

Then in his fluent Mandarin Chinese Stanley would begin to preach, demonstrating, with the aid of his posters or his pictorial presentations on the flannelgraph board, the plight of the human race apart from the mercy and intervention of God. Many times Stanley delighted to use illustrations for his messages from the written characters that make up the Chinese language, for at root Chinese is a pictorial language. The character for the word 'righteousness' is formed by the symbol for a lamb, placed over the symbol that means 'man'.

So, Stanley would tell his hearers, 'the Lamb [of God] covering me [the sinner]' is the only way in which we may be reconciled to God.

A number would follow Stanley back to the mission compound. Some showed genuine interest in his message, many were more concerned about what the white man might give them. Out of her supply of second-hand clothes Norah would help the very poor who had little to wear besides rags. Many were sick, and very often the missionaries could supply rudimentary medicines; others would invite Stanley out to some distant village to preach and teach. Such opportunities were highly valued, and before long Stanley could be seen taking his old bicycle out of the shed and setting off along the dusty cart track, his preaching aids carefully strapped on the back of his bicycle. Bumping along the roads, he would often pass villagers on their way to some distant location. None would be allowed to proceed without a tract from Stanley's ever-ready stock. Few of these people would be literate, but inevitably when they reached their journey's end they would search out someone who could read and so the printed page served a dual purpose and brought the gospel message to many scattered villages.

Back at the mission station, there would be a daily round of gatherings for prayer and instruction. A Chinese prayer meeting is a noisy, awesome event, with each man and woman pouring out his or her heart in prayer, audibly and simultaneously: everyone utterly intent on personal communion with God, and intercession for the needs of life. Norah had many opportunities to visit the women in their homes to teach and pray with them, and to bring advice and help for those in dire need. Little children were often ill and Norah, remembering her own helpless distress as she had

A typical Chinese town in the 1940s

watched her sick baby die, did all she could to alleviate the suffering. There were also many opportunities to teach the children. No well-ordered Sunday school classes these: crying babies, chickens pecking around for crumbs, and even the odd donkey adding to the general confusion, made consistent teaching difficult. Yet despite it all, many children did hear and understand the rudiments of the Christian message, seed well-sown that would bear fruit in later years.

The first sign that someone had given serious attention to the Christian message was evidenced in the householder's willingness to remove and sometimes destroy the family idols, erected in many a crevice of his home. Ostensibly to protect and prosper the people's lives, these paper gods in reality kept them in the bondage of superstition and fear. Most venerated the spirits of their ancestors, and to turn from such worship appeared a violation of their duty as well as an invitation for the vengeance of the spirits to be visited on their homes and families.

But all this intense activity on the part of my parents meant that I often found myself with much time on my own.

One of the single lady missionaries on the station began teaching me to read, together with some elementary number work, but mostly I either played with my Chinese friends, cared for my pet rabbits, or wandered around alone. Even when she was not busy with some of her many missionary duties, my mother often seemed preoccupied. To my perspective she appeared uninterested in her child's needs, often with her head in some book. Had I been older I might have understood that the sorrows my mother had endured were perhaps at the root of such apparent lack of concern in her remaining child. Nor did I realize that she often felt far from well, and especially as she was now pregnant once more.

The mission station was composed of an open courtyard, not dissimilar to a Roman atrium in style, protected by a gate from the public street beyond. Many rooms opened off the courtyard some on to a balcony that ran along the back of the complex. These units formed the living accommodation for individual missionaries, the servants' quarters where my young friends lived, kitchens, and a chapel where preaching services were held. Frequently a dog, never regarded as a pet in that part of China, would roam the premises at night, to the certain discomfort of any would-be intruders.

Without anyone to prevent me, I would frequently steal out unnoticed from the mission compound and into the hard mud-baked streets of the town. There I would watch the busy population at work. 'Coolies' hurried along carrying their goods skilfully slung from a pliable bamboo pole across their shoulders; stall holders shouted their wares for sale; beggars, pitifully dressed in little but rags, sat in many doorways. Many were the ugly sights and sounds that I inadvertently witnessed and heard. Without the facility of an abattoir for butchering animals intended for meat, locals would carry out such procedures outside their own front doors. I would run in horror as I heard the piteous cries of sheep being slaughtered in the street.

On one occasion I saw a crowd passing the outer gate of my compound home. Shouts and cries arrested my interest and moments later I had slipped out of the gate unobserved and began to follow the crowd. Then I noticed that one man was being dragged along in the middle of the melee and I could see he was weeping and begging for mercy. I did not know at the time, but this was a public execution in progress. Mingling with the mob, I soon found myself outside the town gates. The crowd formed itself into a vast semi-circle. At the far end was one forlorn figure still kneeling and crying out for clemency. At what point I realised just what I was witnessing, I could never afterwards remember. But the sound of the gunshot and the sight of the crumpled figure as it slumped earthward was an image I have never been quite able to erase from my memory.

Summer days were long and hot, and I ran shoeless across the hard mud of the compound yard. The Chinese women clicked their tongues and pointed at my bare feet, for the danger of treading on a scorpion, with potentially disastrous results, was a real one. The winter days were bitter – so cold that one's powers of endurance were tested to the utmost. Even with a padded Chinese gown, the subzero temperatures and biting winds ate into hands and feet. But there were compensations. At Christmas time my father delighted his young daughter by showing me how to make an ice lantern. Into a bucket of water left to freeze overnight, a red-hot poker was plunged. Unfrozen water from the centre ran out and in the cavity left behind a candle was carefully inserted. Two more holes were made in the top of the lantern, and string inserted. As the ice lantern hung by the back door I gazed fascinated by the glow of candlelight through the ice casting distorted shadows all around.

Happy enough in my childish way, I also learned regrettable habits from my Chinese friends. Lying and stealing became routine, as my companions would dare me to raid the larder in my mother's kitchen and bring them out bread and other commodities – for food was often in short supply in their homes. With a jersey bulging with a hidden loaf, I would receive a rapturous welcome from my hungry friends.

News of Christopher was scarce, for letters could rarely be carried safely across war-torn China, vast areas of which were now in Japanese hands. Then, in July 1944, our family celebrated the birth of another son – Philip, doubly precious because of the loss of Godfrey almost ten months earlier. Once more Norah had a small life to nurture and Philip's arrival brought a measure of consolation to our missionary family. But even as I shared in the joy over the birth of my new baby brother, I learned that the day was very close when I too must leave the familiar surrounding of home and make the long trek to Kiating to join Christopher at his boarding school. Late in August our journey was to begin. Stretching out pleading arms in useless protest, I was lifted on to the lorry that would take me, accompanied by my father, for the initial stages of the lengthy journey to Kiating – away from all that I had known in my short life. Baby Philip was just a month old: when would I see him or my home again? I did not know. I was, however, delighted to see my older brother, Christopher, again and to hear of his exploits since he had left home almost two years earlier.

4

ESCAPE FROM THE JAPANESE

Like most other children in such circumstances, I accepted my situation and settled quickly into the new environment, making satisfactory progress with my lessons. It was a small community with twenty-seven children as boarders, and a skeleton staff of five who, owing to the circumstances, were mainly unskilled either as teachers or in the art of caring for children. Some were kindly and anxious to comfort homesick children and to relieve the acute sense of isolation so often evident among their young pupils. But others, who had come to China on the understanding that they were giving their lives for evangelistic work among the Chinese, undoubtedly felt frustrated – even resentful. Instead of fulfilling their desired calling, they had been sent by the directors of the mission to an out-of-the-way spot for the mundane task of caring for the children of their fellow missionaries. Consequently, as I would soon discover, one or two were unnecessarily heavy-handed, even harsh, in their dealings with the pupils.

Many small children, disturbed by the sudden loss of parents and home, showed their distress by becoming bed-wetters. These unfortunate children were obliged to have a notice posted at the head of their beds that read in large letters, 'I am a baby. I wet my bed.' What today's child psychologists would have made of such an elementary blunder, it is hard to say. I looked on in pity, only too glad that I myself did not come into that category and suffer a like ignominy.

Even though the school had been sited in a part of China thought to be safe from Japanese incursion, the situation was becoming steadily more troubling. The Japanese conquest of vast areas of Burma, and their success in cutting off the Burma Road at its source during 1942, left the school in a vulnerable position. The Burma Road, built in 1938–39 after the Japanese occupation of China's eastern sea ports, was a vital supply line, running from Lashio in Burma, to Kunming in Yunnan province.[1] Food and vital resources came into China along that route, together with a supply of aircraft and other munitions from America to aid the Chinese war effort.

December 1944 has been described as among the darkest months in all China's long history. Despite the fact of the crushing defeat of the Japanese forces six months earlier by General Sir William Slim at the Battle of Kohima in northeast India, not far from the Burmese border – a battle which left 30,000 Japanese dead and marked a turning point in their war effort – daily rumours still told of advancing armies in parts of Free China. By the end of November the Japanese had thrust back the Nationalist forces as far as Kweiyang, only two hundred miles south of Chongqing (Chungking), Chiang Kai-shek's war time capital. After having secured a vital railhead that linked up with the Burma Road, the

---

[1] After the war the road was extended to Chongqing, but later fell into disuse when the New Burma Road was opened.

Japanese then pressed on as far as Nanning, another strategic town yet further south.

Chongqing itself, where the China Inland Mission had also established its headquarters after the fall of Shanghai, was now coming under continual aerial bombardment as the hostile forces drew ever closer to this mountain fortress. Meanwhile, at the school in Kiating food supplies were running severely short – no one knew how much longer the town could stand. Situated on an important waterway, the River Min, it would be a prime target for the Japanese war effort. The staff at the school, carrying the heavy responsibility of making decisions on behalf of the children of their fellow missionaries, were clearly deeply troubled. They scarcely knew what to do for the best. Should they attempt to evacuate the whole school to some safer country? Should they stay where they were in hope that an Allied victory, looking ever more likely as 1944 wore to its weary end, might put an end to Japanese advances. Wisely they shielded the children from any news of the imminent danger, but I could not help noticing the ever-increasing grave looks passing between them and the whispered consultations as they weighed up the options. And still the enemy forces advanced.

It was almost Christmas, 1944. I had been at school for three months, but for none of the staff or children would there be any time or opportunity to celebrate Christmas that year. Provisional plans for escape had been drawn up, boxes of school equipment packed, and still the staff watched and waited. Then came a decision, and not a moment too soon, for the enemy forces were approaching the very gates of Kiating. A message from the mission headquarters in Chongqing ordered the immediate evacuation of the school to India. But time was at a premium because Chongqing itself and its airport were in imminent danger. The severe bombing by enemy aircraft meant that the town could fall at any moment, closing one of the last escape routes out of the country. Knowing full well the fate of the other half of the school, facing a third year in an internment camp now in Weihsien, all plans were finalized: the school would be evacuated the very next day.

Still we were told nothing. However, very early the following morning we were all roused from our beds, told to dress immediately in as many layers of clothing as possible; we could choose two toys that we wished to take with us, and then must report without delay to the dining room. There, over hot mugs of cocoa, the situation was explained to us. As yet enemy intelligence appeared to be unaware that English and American children were in the town of Kiating. Our escape must be immediate, or we too might face internment, or even torture, at the hands of a ruthless force.

As we sat at the tables nursing our empty mugs, a member of staff read to us from Psalm 91. For the second time in my life eternal things became very real to me:

> He who dwells in the secret place of the Most High shall abide under the shadow of the Almighty. I will say of the LORD, 'He is my refuge and my fortress; my God, in him will I trust.' . . . He shall cover you with his feathers and under his wings you shall trust . . . He shall give his angels charge over you, to keep you in all your ways . . .

If God had promised to protect his people long ago, he would not let any harm come to us now, I reasoned. So it was with a mixture of excitement and wonder that I filed out with the other children, and there discovered two American army lorries – big ones with ten wheels apiece, we noted in amazement – waiting for us. They were already packed with box after box of luggage, so that there scarcely seemed room for us. But one by one we were lifted in, twelve or more children in each vehicle.

As the lorries rumbled through the deserted streets of the town, we children could hardly contain our excitement, but the accompanying members of staff were nervy and silent. We must reach the airport without delay, and a long journey lay ahead through rough terrain – it could take several days. It was not much more than a hundred and fifty miles to Chongqing, but progress was severely hampered, for we were not the only ones on the move. The road was thronged with refugees, desperate, starving people, with only one priority: to find some place of safety. All carried their few worldly possessions with them, and as they stumbled along, strained and suffering faces told their own story. Women with bound feet struggled to carry loads beyond their physical strength, reports of Japanese cruelty in captured towns and cities goading them ever onwards. And every now and then enemy aircraft roared overhead, shooting at random into the struggling column. As the distant thunder of an approaching plane grew louder we cowered in fear, but no shots penetrated our canvas-topped lorries. And still we crawled along, unable to make much significant progress. Always the frightening though unspoken question was whether or not the airport would still be open by the time we arrived. Or would we be driving straight into enemy hands?

The Sino-Japanese war was not a conflict in isolation. Following the attack on Pearl Harbour in December 1941, Malaya, the Philippines, Burma, Singapore had also come under Japanese domination, and it was even possible that

India might be the next target. It was crucial to the Allied war effort to strengthen Chinese resistance and thereby help to contain Japan's seemingly unremitting advance in the Pacific. U.S. Army and Air Force units were therefore posted at many airfields in Free China to ensure they remained open.

As night fell, the lorries carrying the school children stopped at an American airbase, to the delight of the young escapees. Travel weary, frightened and sometimes unwell, we were grateful to climb down from the cramped lorries. The American airmen were delighted to entertain the fugitives. Some of the boys were invited to inspect the American bombers and even climb into the cockpit. Far from their homes and families at Christmas time, the airmen were trying to enjoy the festive season as best they could, and escaping youngsters gave them an excuse for further celebrations. A Christmas dinner was laid on for the travellers at each American airbase en route, as Christopher and I later recollected, although neither of us had any appetite for it. The thought of Christmas pudding, together with the haunting smell of chewing gum, so popular with the Americans, has remained forever in my mind, invariably connected with that flight from danger.

Earnest prayer had been offered by local Chinese Christians and missionaries alike that the Japanese onslaught on the cities of the west, and Chongqing in particular, might be halted. And it was a prayer God was pleased to answer. The early snows of winter had hampered Japanese progress and, although advanced forces made threatening sorties as far as the airport perimeter, in fact, Chongqing itself never fell into Japanese hands. Called the 'Mountain City', old Chongqing was built on the steep surrounding mountains, at the meeting point of two great waterways: China's longest river, the Yangtze, and the Jialing river. These geographical features had proved of vital importance in the defence of the city.

With the closure of the vital supply routes along the Burma Road and any way of exit from the country by means of the eastern sea ports, the American Air Force had pioneered a new air route from China into India flying across 'the Hump', as the eastern end of the Himalayan range was dubbed. With aircraft of that time unable to gain the flying altitudes commonplace today, the attempt to clear mountains that reached a phenomenal 20,000 feet was exceptionally hazardous. The extreme air turbulence at such altitudes had resulted in many aircraft being lost as they attempted to cross the Hump. But there was no alternative. In addition, the oxygen supply at those heights was so thin that any one suffering from breathing difficulties was at grave risk. Without pressurized cabins, the flight was far from comfortable.

Christmas Day 1944! At last we had arrived at the airport without serious incident. From Chongqing we would fly to Kunming in the province of Yunnan. There the plane would refuel, and from Kunming the school was to make the hazardous flight across the Hump into Calcutta in India. On our arrival, however, confusion seemed to reign as arguments broke out among Chinese airport officials as to which plane we were supposed to be travelling in. The hours crawled by and as we waited yet another Christmas dinner was served up. Night fell, but conditions were too dangerous for lights to be turned on, especially as Japanese soldiers had been sighted on the perimeter of the airport.

With problems finally resolved we climbed back into the lorries to cross the tarmac to a small military DC-3 aircraft waiting at a distance, shrouded in darkness. One by one we were lifted from the lorry, passed along a silent row of American soldiers, and dropped unceremoniously into what appeared to us to be a black hole, but was actually the door of the aeroplane. Here we settled down on metal seats that lined both walls, facing a mountain of cargo boxes stacked along the centre. 'Duck down, all of you,' a member of staff said urgently. Obediently we all ducked so that no face appeared at the windows to tell of our presence. Then with a burst of power the small plane shot off down the runway and roared skyward. Japanese intelligence was oblivious to the fact that some thirty or more American and English children and adults had just become airborne.

Unaware of the dangers we faced, we children regarded the journey as an adventure. Little did we realize how close we would come to disaster. After a two-hour flight the aircraft approached Kunming airport, where it would need to refuel. Then came radio signals telling of an imminent bombing raid on the airport. It would be impossible to land. All radio signals were cut off, for incoming bombers could also pick up the signals. Without any guidance the pilot circled helplessly round and round for a further two hours until all bearings were lost. And still there was no communication from the ground to guide us to safety. Now fuel was running drastically short.

Not primarily intended for passenger flights, the aircraft carried no parachutes, and as time passed the accompanying staff realized, although we did not, that our situation was critical. With tanks almost empty the pilot knew he would have to attempt an emergency landing, but where could he land? He faced the appalling prospect of having to crash-land his machine, probably killing all his young passengers and himself too. At that critical moment contact was restored with the ground and the despairing pilot was given instructions to land at Yunnani, a nearby emergency airfield, where it might prove possible to bring the aircraft down safely. As he prepared to land, his fuel supply ran completely dry – not a drop was left. The only option remaining was to attempt to glide-land the plane – a desperate expedient. Guided by airport staff, and beyond all expectations, the pilot managed the manoeuvre and, after a bumpy landing, the plane shuddered to a standstill. The children were safe, but the effect of the trauma on the pilot himself was serious. Rumour had it that, after the journey to India was accomplished, he never flew again.

Refuelled, the aircraft took off once more, and soon landed safely in Kunming where a 2.00 am breakfast served with typical American generosity was enjoyed by the hungry passengers. But still the dangerous crossing of the Hump lay ahead. With ears popping as our plane roared into the air once more, we were thrown to and fro as we gradually gained height. Just turned seven years of age at the time, I have few recollections of that eventful journey, and little wonder, for the extreme shortage of oxygen had a soporific effect on all the young passengers. But I can remember seeing one of my friends, a Swedish boy who suffered from asthma, in serious difficulty. Panic quickly spread among us as Ralph was being given emergency oxygen. Palpable relief marked the faces of the members of staff as the 'Hump' was cleared at last. Breathing became easier as the altitude decreased. Calcutta gradually loomed larger and clearer beneath us and the aircraft was brought safely to rest.

In later years I recollected the words of the Psalm that had been read to us before that precarious journey began and knew then that God had indeed been 'a refuge and a fortress' to us – my trust was not misplaced.

The heat, bustle and noise of Calcutta made an unforgettable impression on the children as we bundled down the flight steps, scarcely able to take in the sudden change of circumstances. Far into the hot night my mind was racing as I lay wakeful among the rows of sleeping children, hastily accommodated in a refugee centre upon arrival. Did our parents know that their children were now far off in India? Would I ever see them again? Would Philip ever learn that he had a sister and a brother? Where were we going? I did not know the answers. And still sleep refused to come. Apprehensively I lay there listening to the sound of distant vehicles as they drove past. At least someone else in the world must still be awake, I decided, drawing a shred of comfort from the thought. At last sleep enveloped a wakeful child, and with it relief and oblivion.

5

A SCHOOL IN EXILE

After some time in Calcutta, arrangements were in place for the school to be accommodated in two cottage homes near Kalimpong, far up in the foothills of the Himalayas, above Darjeeling. Lying some three hundred miles north of Calcutta, and more than 7,000 feet above sea level, Darjeeling is situated on a long narrow mountain ridge of the Sikkim Himalayas that climbs steeply upwards from the Great Rangit River basin. The area is one where many would-be climbers of Everest must wait to become acclimatized before beginning their hopeful ascent.

These vacant children's homes, known as the Dr Graham Homes, had been generously loaned to the China Inland Mission to accommodate the school for as long as necessary. Nestling under the shadow of the eastern Himalayan range, and with a commanding view across the Indian hills stretching away into the distance, they had been built as part of the St Andrew's Homes complex to care for Anglo-Indian orphans; they included a number of other homes, together with a church, a bakery, and similar amenities.

A train from Calcutta, crowded to capacity, took us on the first stage of our journey. Hours passed and still the train rattled and swayed until eventually we reached a remote station where we had to change to a narrow gauge railway to take us far up the mountainside to Kalimpong. We stared in disbelief at the waiting train with its miniature steam engine and tiny carriages, looking like something straight out of Enid Blyton's *Toytown*, and learned that it was to carry us yet further upwards to our unknown home. Along precipitous mountain tracks the small engine puffed and shook, gathering speed on the straight, slowing on the corners, as it zigzagged steadily upwards, ever higher and higher. Kalimpong at last came into sight; here we alighted, for the railway went no further, and piling into several trucks, soon left the small market town behind.

Up and up we crawled, the road still winding on above us, until we reached a point where it deteriorated into a gravel track. From here we had to walk the last half mile or so, picking our way in single file as we followed the coolies who carried the luggage.

At last we reached the grassy slopes where the St Andrew's Homes were situated. Further up the hillside, and at some distance from the other homes, stood the cottage loaned to the mission where we would sleep in several large dormitories. Some way down the hillside we could just pick out the roof of the second cottage where we would eat and have our lessons.

Delightfully cool after the oppression of Calcutta, it was an idyllic spot and we settled down quickly in our new mountain home. From our high vantage point we could look out at night and see the lights of Darjeeling twinkling in the black sky far below us. Strange unearthly night cries puzzled us at first until we learnt that they were from jackals out foraging for food. Rumours of tigers roaming the hills excited and scared us. Much of our time was spent out of doors and odd-looking Indian insects fascinated us. I gained short-lived popularity when I discovered a particularly rare one, wrinkled, brown and six inches long, but it did not approve of the diet of leaves I provided and soon died.

The responsibility for such a group of children in difficult circumstances brought a pressure on the staff which often left them touchy and nervous. A strict regime of discipline was therefore imposed on the children. In war conditions it was difficult to obtain new clothes and shoes for growing youngsters, so the necessity of taking extra care was strongly emphasized. There were daily inspections of both clothes and footwear and regular corporal punishment was administered for any perceived carelessness.

Before long an Indian seamstress was engaged to make new clothes for us and soon the boys had the appearance of a small army of soldiers each clad in khaki jackets and matching shorts. All eighteen girls were given dresses of similar design with slight variations in style, made of blue checked material. Harder to replace than dresses and shorts were our shoes and these needed to be preserved for as long as possible so that outgrown footwear could be passed down to younger children. So for most of the time we were quite happy to work and play barefooted like the Indian children of the villages around. Little feet grew brown and tough, impervious to stones.

Our shoes were reserved for special occasions and for Sundays when the school lined up in crocodile fashion and marched off to the St Andrew's Homes church. Here we joined others, many of them Indian children living in these homes, for a united service conducted in Anglican style, complete with surplices and robed Indian choir boys – a strange experience for us.

When the monsoon rains fell, water from the overflowing streams cascaded down the gullies in the mountainside, and we delighted to paddle in the cool brown waters. During the heat of summer, meals were served from a long table running in front of one of the homes. Nor were we the only ones to be enjoying an outdoor meal; sometimes we would watch in astonishment as a flock of vultures descended noisily on the carcass of some unfortunate recently-killed animal, perhaps a hyena or a jackal. Ripping the creature to pieces with their long talons, they would feast greedily, scarcely leaving a bone behind. So satiated were the vultures after their meal that they could hardly get airborne again.

News from China was limited and unreliable, and letters between parents and children irregular at best. Toys were also unobtainable, but soon we began to manufacture our own games. Stones gathered from the hillside were carefully laid out to form aeroplanes. A privileged child would climb into the 'cockpit' and all the others would be his passengers on many a long distance 'flight'. Hospital beds were also constructed from stones with a 'patient' lying in each, while another child would take the part of the doctor or nurse.

Books too were scarce. With so few available I would read each story many times over until I could recite some books by heart. When the story of *Lobo, the Lone Wolf*, was read aloud to us – a narrative telling of an animal hunted mercilessly until it met its death from the huntsman's gun – I found the narrative gripping and moving. If only I could keep that book as my very own! Then I could read it again and again. My most precious possession at that time was a small bookmark I had recently plaited out of coloured cottons. Perhaps the teacher would accept the bookmark in exchange for *Lobo, the Lone Wolf*. Not surprisingly the offer was gently refused.

The days might well have been happy enough, had not the constant anxiety arising from our circumstances and uncertainty as to the duration of the war unnerved and troubled some members of staff. The tensions they faced, and the frustrations of spending their days caring for other people's children, often led to discipline which was heavy-handed and unjust. The master, who combined the function of caretaker with one of special responsibility for the boys, found that my brother, Christopher, a mischievous lad by nature, was giving him many a problem. As a result the boy was regularly and severely chastised for his misdemeanours. Meanwhile, I was having equal difficulties trying to please the caretaker's red-headed wife who acted as matron and nurse.

Supplies of new material for our clothes became increasingly hard to obtain and it became ever more important that all garments should be cared for and wear and tear eliminated at all costs. This seemed an almost impossible standard from my childish perspective. Careless by nature, I found it difficult to worry about such things – and was frequently punished for many childish peccadilloes: torn dresses, lost buttons and handkerchiefs, or broken elastic were regular offences. With much of my father's love of adventure in my blood, I often discovered myself on a collision course with the matron. An irresistible urge to clamber up rocks, climb trees or wade across mountain streams inevitably led to trouble. Because of the problems such mishaps generated, punishments far outweighed the misdeed.

As the months wore on the punishments grew harsher and we were well aware that we were being unjustly treated. On the night of my eighth birthday, as I was lying in bed, I began to colour a small flat stick, the size of a lollipop stick – a birthday gift from a friend. Inadvertently I not only coloured the stick but managed to mark the sheet with green crayon as well. When the offending green lines were noticed on my sheet in the morning, retribution was swift and merciless. I begged the matron for forgiveness, protesting that the offence had been a mistake. 'Then I shall strap you by mistake', was the heartless reply, as she ordered me to bend across the 'punishment trunk'. As a result there were long bruises up my legs marking where the belt had struck. Even the imprints of the buckle were discernible on my thighs. The following day, with total naivety and little understanding of the possible consequences, I joined the queue of children who required some medical attention. When my turn came I displayed my bruises and asked for cream to alleviate the pain. Not surprisingly such audacity very nearly brought me more of the same.

Such treatment of the children is corroborated by others who were also in Kalimpong at the same time. One former pupil refers to 'repeated spankings over a trunk with a belt' which for her became 'a weekly performance'; while another writes, 'I can remember a time once when someone was being thrashed (always with a leather belt) and it went on and on. We were very upset and shouted for it to stop. We could hear it through the door as this took place in a little room leading off the dormitory where you had to lean over a trunk while they administered the punishment.' The girl in this case was also badly bruised in consequence.

This inequitable treatment turned my mind to the Saviour about whom I had been taught from earliest days. He too had been unjustly treated, and although I knew that such comparisons were invalid for he had never sinned, thoughts of him brought both consolation and the power to forgive. On one occasion, I came across a hymn. I had never heard it sung, but the words, speaking of the death of Jesus Christ on Calvary, enduring punishment that he did not deserve, touched me deeply. Surely, he knew my sorrows. I learnt the hymn by heart:

> Alas! and did my Saviour bleed?
> And did my Sovereign die?
> Would he devote that sacred head
> For such a worm as I?
>
> Was it for crimes that I had done
> He groaned upon the tree?
> Amazing pity! grace unknown!
> And love beyond degree!

Such love, such compassion demanded a response, and it was with a childish sincerity that I repeated the final words:

> But drops of grief can ne'er repay
> The debt of love I owe;
> Here, Lord, I give myself away;
> 'Tis all that I can do.
> *Isaac Watts, 1674–1748*

I began to learn passages of Scripture by heart, and again it was the account of the sufferings and death of Christ that attracted me. I soon mastered much of Matthew 27, and a few passages from the Psalms.

Unfortunately, side by side with such desires went other less attractive characteristics as I continued to steal and lie, usually in an attempt to avoid the punishments that I feared might be coming. Once I crept into the matron's workroom and cut a length of new elastic in order to replace some I had broken – a desperate though unsuccessful ploy to stay clear of trouble – and one that brought its own just reprisals. If it were discovered that children had lied about some misdemeanour we would be required to rinse our mouths out with salt water, or sometimes soap and water, to 'cleanse' them from the contamination of lying.

By no means all, or even most, of the staff acted with any harshness towards the children. Indeed, some punishments were less severe than the offence deserved. When my friend and I decided to pull the wings off sleepy flies, the member of staff whose special responsibility it was to teach nature study,

Taken for my eighth birthday.

was horrified. Such cruelty in small children needed to be checked at once, and she quickly found a fur-lined slipper – a fact I noted with relief – with which to administer justice: a lesson well-deserved and long remembered.

Many of the staff were concerned for the welfare and happiness of the children in their care. Unable to compensate for the loss of parental love, they tried to observe signs of distress. I had always feared sudden loud noises, even from the days when the bombs were falling on London. Now I found the tropical thunderstorms terrifying. The name of nearby Darjeeling can be literally translated 'place of the thunderbolt', a name given to the town no doubt because of the fearsome roar of the thunder as it reverberated all around the surrounding mountains. During a storm the skies would be lit up with fierce orange light, and the whole building seem to rock and tremble as one crash followed upon another. One night a member of staff discovered the frightened child cowering under the bedclothes. Taking me to the window, she told me to look out at the sky. As I did so, unwillingly at first but then with growing confidence, I saw the strong mountains illuminated in bold silhouette against the orange sky as a sheet of lightning banished the dark of night. Then followed an eerie blackness. It was a breathtaking sight – splendid and mysterious. The teacher explained that even in the awesome storms there was a beauty that marked each aspect of nature as God's handiwork. Gradually I lost my fear.

One treat the children sometimes enjoyed on a clear day was a short early morning walk up a nearby hill where we could watch the sun rising over Kanchenjunga. The world's third highest mountain, Kanchenjunga soars to a breathtaking 28,169 feet, and the sight of the sun turning its snowy peaks to pinks and reds, the clouds circling its heights like a skirt, was unforgettable. On a clear day it was possible, or so we were told, to obtain spectacular views of Mount Everest itself a hundred miles off in the distance.

Like any other young child taken from the security of her home and parents, I craved attention. Among the youngest in the school, my homesickness was often acute; then I would cry quietly into my pillow at night, longing for my father's loud cheery voice or my mother's goodnight kiss. The only way to obtain such individual care was through illness. For some months I had been suffering from recurring fevers; I made the most of these and some of my frequent complaints were, in fact, exaggerated in order to gain the sympathy for which I longed. As no one could discover the root of my trouble I found myself transferred at last to the Kalimpong hospital. Whether any problem was diagnosed at the time, I never knew; enough for me that one night I saw a spider of terrifying proportions – its body three inches in diameter and its hairy legs each six inches long – creeping down the wall and disappearing under my bed. The sight certainly cured my ailments, at least temporarily, and a sudden 'recovery' meant I was speedily taken back to the school.

In August 1945 came the devastating atomic bombs that precipitated Japan's capitulation and the final end to World War II. Victory flares beamed out across the night sky and the sense of jubilation percolated through to the exiles far away in the Indian mountains. Our circumstances had been ideal in some respects, far from the noise and fear of war, but young hearts longed to see their parents once more and hoped they might soon be able to return to China. In the event it was not until June 1946 that final arrangements for the return journey were in place. Eighteen months had passed since that dramatic flight from the advancing Japanese army.

First the school left its mountain retreat in Kalimpong and returned to Calcutta. Once again the blistering heat affected staff and children alike, leaving all enervated and often bad tempered. A small hotel was found to accommodate the school until transport to Shanghai could be arranged. In vain the staff struggled to provide some form of normality by sitting the children side by side on the beds and attempting to conduct lessons as usual. But when young and old developed prickly heat rashes the effort was abandoned.

The return journey was to be by sea: the boys were taken first, accompanied by their master. As they travelled Christopher once more drew down the wrath of the teacher upon himself for some act of disobedience. The punishment was a harsh one: his most prized possession – and the boy had little enough that he could call his own – a small penknife, was thrown overboard. Had more appropriate appointments been made to fill the position of the school caretaker and his wife, the children would have looked back on the days in India with much happier memories.

A little later the girls followed on in a small coasting vessel. As we crossed the choppy waters of the Bay of Bengal, through the Straits of Malacca and out into the China Sea, I was overcome with sea-sickness, as were most of the other young passengers and even the adults. The long hot voyage took a month and conditions on board were primitive. Only one pint of water a day had to suffice for all washing purposes for three or four children. It was with relief, then, that we eventually disembarked in Shanghai, where transport waited to take us through bomb-damaged streets to the mission headquarters in Sinza Road, now restored to the mission following the Japanese withdrawal.

6

IN TROUBLE
WITH RATS

After eighteen months with little medical care it was important that all the children had check-ups for any sign of disease. In accordance with the medical thought of the day, it was decided that most of the pupils would need their tonsils removed, and so were taken to the mission hospital in groups for the operation. I had unhappy memories of my period in an Indian hospital, and was nervous when my turn came for surgery, but my recollection afterwards was nothing but a very sore throat, understandable in the circumstances. Clearer was the memory of the day I contracted mumps only a few weeks later. With mischievous glee I had made an 'apple-pie bed' for one of the other children. But when the unhappy victim found that her legs became stuck halfway down her bed, she was not pleased and complained to the matron. I was in certain trouble. Having been promised a belting in the morning, I lay awake pondering any means of escape, for I had good reason to know what such punishment meant. A mumps epidemic was spreading among the children and I earnestly hoped, even prayed, that I might catch the infection in time to save me from the threatened punishment.

'Have I got mumps?' I demanded of the child in the next bed as soon as the other awoke in the morning. My relief knew no bounds when the reply, based on my swollen face, was in the affirmative, and I was escorted off to the sanatorium. Never had mumps been more welcome.

As soon as it was possible in post-war China, messages were sent to all the parents telling them that their children were at last safely back in the country. Great were the celebrations at the news in far-off Tianshui, some three hundred miles south of Lanzhou, in the province of Gansu, where Stanley and Norah were currently stationed. Almost four years had elapsed since they had seen ten-year-old Christopher. To me, two years had seemed a long enough time. Without delay Stanley prepared for the journey to Shanghai to collect us, and bring us to Tianshui for the summer months.

'Would someone introduce me to my father?' asked Christopher in a bewildered voice as the boy learnt that Stanley had arrived. It was a shy though joyful reunion and without further delay the family set off on the long journey home. Remembering his daughter's love for living things, my father had bought me a small pet to care for – a chipmunk of my very own. I made the little creature a comfortable bed by turning up the bottom edge of my jersey so that it could sleep securely as we travelled. Day after day we bumped along on the back of an open lorry, or took advantage of an occasional train still functioning despite the miles of tracks blasted away by enemy action.

Each night the journey was broken at some wayside inn. The inn was a bustle of noise and activity – the yard a menagerie of living things. Hens pecked among the rubbish for scraps of grain, geese hissed angrily at every disturbance, donkeys brayed as the panniers containing their burden of commodities for sale at some market were lifted from their backs. Mules munched contentedly at the piles of hay provided. But for Christopher and me the most intriguing sight was of the camels, resting from their day's journey. This was a method of travel favoured by business men, quicker and safer from bandits than the slow-jogging mule carts. Some of the animals knelt down to rest for the night, quietly masticating their provender. Others remained standing, raising their proud heads and snorting impatiently. They seemed less than friendly towards their young visitors, as indeed they were – and as Christopher was to find when one vicious beast kicked out at him. All his life he was to carry a scar from the wound he received.

But one night as I sat eating my supper at an inn table, plying my chopsticks deftly over a bowl of rice or *mien* enhanced by a variety of meats and vegetables, as I had learned to do before going to school, a tragedy (from my perspective) occurred. The chipmunk which had accompanied me on my journey suddenly spotted his chance to escape. With a quick leap he bolted from my jersey and disappeared down a rat hole. I was distressed at the loss. Call and cajole as I might, I could not retrieve my pet. He appeared to prefer the company of the rats to his comfortable bed in my upturned jersey.

A break in the journey at the mission headquarters in Xi-an (Sian) was a welcome relief for the travel-weary family. We had already been on the road for many days and here was the luxury of a proper bed at night and, even more, the provision of running water for washing. Xi-an, capital city in the province of Shaanxi, with a present population of some two and a half million, is now a favourite venue for tourists.

They come from all over the world to see the strange army of six thousand terracotta figures to be found twenty miles north-east of the city. Excavated in 1974 in a tomb of some long forgotten dignitary, they were there ostensibly to guard him through all the hazards of an unknown eternity. In the 1940s, however, Xi-an was a city of major importance in the Chinese economy and, with its shifting, needy population, an obvious centre for the work of the missionaries.

During that long trek back to north-west China by train, lorry and mule-cart, I wondered about my mother. My memory of her was faint. Would I even recognize her? What was she like? Would I love her? I scarcely knew the answers. After several weeks of travel we reached Tianshui at last, and a few moments dispelled all my fears about my mother. Norah hugged her small daughter as if she could never let me go again. Then began the long process of getting to know each other once more. Shyness proved a barrier not easily overcome, but my delight in my young brother Philip, now turned two, and a delightful toddler with a thatch of fair hair and bright blue eyes, was unbounded.

Gradually both Christopher and I settled back into the routine of life at the mission station. Our command of Chinese, unused since we had left for school, quickly returned. But although I had coped with many problems in the intervening years, I met another in Tianshui that proved almost too much. Rats. The place was infested with rats. One night my father set a trap for the unwelcome invaders, luring them to their death as they jumped up into a large container of honey, and then tumbled back into a bucket of water. At least thirty perished that night. But the communal toilets, large open pits in the yard with two planks across, filled me with unimaginable panic. Peering into the murky depths I could invariably see shining rat eyes looking up at me or catch a glimpse of the quick whisk of a tail as a rodent disappeared from view. And when I found small paw marks in the thick yellow loess dust that blew in from the desert, marking a trail across the furniture in my bedroom, my panic rose to a new height. My parents had no alternative but to make up a small bed for me in the corner of their room.

Added to this, my parents noticed that I seemed unaccountably lethargic. Was there something wrong with their eight-year-old? Instead of racing around with Christopher or amusing my small brother, I sat doing little. But when they discovered that I could not run even a few paces without exhaustion they became deeply troubled. Perhaps all the complaints while the school was in India had a basis in reality.

Towards the middle of September 1946, my father escorted Christopher and me back to Shanghai. The school was due to reopen for the autumn term, this time at the mission headquarters, until alternative accommodation could be found. The wrench of separation was not so acute now, because our family would shortly be returning to England for a break following the regular seven year period on the mission field.

Not long after reaching Shanghai, however, my condition deteriorated sharply. I knew little about it, for a delirious fever obliterated the memory of the early days of my illness. All I could remember was the night I was carried from my bed in the dormitory into an isolation room. There I was to remain for almost two months.

But the rats, the rats – these I did remember, and with terror. My phobia intensified as I discovered that the isolation ward also was rat-infested. Each night as I lay alone I could hear their busy feet scurrying across the floor. Sometimes a particularly adventurous rodent scrambled right on to the bed. Only a frail mosquito net shielded me from its physical presence. Desperation drove me to a variety of expedients to deal with the problem. Forbidden to leave my bed, I decided to attach a string to the light switch; as the nightly incursion of pests began I would pull the string which would turn on the light. The sudden blaze would then drive my tormentors back to their holes. But this ruse was discovered by the nursing staff and prohibited. Another and more successful expedient was that of an old metal hairbrush attached to a string. As the darkness gathered and the pattering of little feet grew louder, I would let down my brush and bang it on the floor. Gratefully I listened as the rats scampered away in alarm.

The cause of my serious illness was not diagnosed at the time, but I made a steady, though slow, recovery. Soon after my ninth birthday, in the late autumn of 1946, I was well enough to travel to Hong Kong with my parents and brothers to begin the long journey to England.

7

A FAMILY TOGETHER

Perhaps at last the family would enjoy a brief spell of life together during the year that lay ahead. A few days were spent in Hong Kong while we awaited a P & O liner to take us on the first stage of the homeward journey. The crowds, bustle, and western-style shops in Hong Kong seemed a new world to me, but for Christopher it was the snake charmers that captivated him most. How could men juggle with the deadly creatures, allowing them to curl around their bodies and flicker long tongues within inches of their faces and yet remain unharmed? We did not know, but Christopher at least had a strong suspicion that, contrary to all that was said, the venomous sting had already been removed.

At last it was time to board the P & O *Canton*, bound for the western seaboard of the United States. As we filed up the gangplank and discovered which cabin would be ours, we could hardly contain our excitement. I clambered to a top bunk and claimed it as my territory while my younger brother Philip was left with the bottom bunk. My mother also shared the same cabin. Pressing my nose against the porthole window, I could watch the endless movement of the sea, while from my own private window in the top bunk I had a

Snake charmers in Hong Kong.

secret vantage point to view the corridor outside. But it was
the luxury that astonished me most of all – I had not seen
anything like it before. Upholstered chairs, carpeted floors,
shining clean glassware and splendid meals, all new to a child
from inland China.

With the Middle East still in turmoil in the aftermath of
the war, it had been decided that the safest way to travel
would be in three stages: first across the Pacific to America;
then a train journey right across America, passing through
mountains and across wide-open plains from San Francisco
to New York; finally there would be a second voyage, this
time across the Atlantic, from New York to Southampton.

The leisurely journey across the Pacific was a highly
pleasurable one to children who had so recently been
deprived of even some of the basic commodities of life. The
swimming pool was a constant centre of attraction and
activity. I could not swim, and my single venture into water
beyond my depth led to immediate trouble, until a kindly
fellow passenger leant over the side with a helping hand. The
sparkling blue of the ocean crested with gleaming white foam

Tourist smoking room on P&O *Canton*

and the occasional sight of distant porpoises acted as a magnet to the young passengers. However, as day followed day, we eventually found the sight of little else but a vast expanse of sea and sky a wearisome one.

At last, with great excitement, we could pick out the magnificent Golden Gate Bridge in the distance: the gateway to America, built only nine years earlier. With its single span stretching for more than 4,000 feet and soaring 265 feet above the water, the bridge was an engineering marvel unsurpassed at that time. The ship's horn boomed out its jubilant greeting as we drew nearer, and we watched in amazement as the great liner, like a toy boat, slipped under the bridge and into San Francisco Bay.

The wonders of a journey across the heart of America were largely lost on Christopher and me, though the thrill of sleeping in bunk beds on a train was not. The train sped ever onward, past the Salt Flats and Salt Lake City, through the rocky canyons, across Buffalo Bill country, and past countless other sights that tourists pay dearly to view, until at last we reached New York.

Accommodation in one of the city's vast apartment blocks was a memorable experience. As the lift sailed on upwards past more floors than we could count, our astonishment grew yet greater. At last we were allocated our rooms, and as we gazed out of the window down to the pavement far below, Christopher decided that the pedestrians might well have been the inhabitants of Gulliver's Lilliput.

The last leg of the journey ended as the ship from New York finally docked at Southampton in January 1947. There, waiting on the quayside to greet us, were a number of previously unknown relatives: aunts, uncles and grandparents, of whom we had no recollection at all. The hugging and handshakes seemed endless, but at last it was over and we were on the train to London where the family would spend time before being allocated to our accommodation for the year.

Soon we were settled in the village of Bidborough in Kent, in a quiet country house belonging to the mission, built in Swiss style and known as *The Chalet*. I was sent to the village school, while Christopher attended a secondary school in nearby Tonbridge. The village school consisted of only one class, where all children of five to eleven years were being taught in a single room, the older children being expected to help the younger ones with their early learning. Miss Gilbert, who managed the school single-handedly, kept her assorted selection of pupils in good order and I soon learnt that I would have to behave myself under the village school-mistress's watchful eye. But I had little incentive for mischief for I was captivated by the books. Never had I seen so many books before! Now I could read to my heart's content. And read I did. While others enjoyed communal games in the playground, I was quite happy to sit inside lost in some exciting story.

The winter of 1946–47 was marked by many food short-ages in Britain. Though the war was over, food rationing became yet more stringent, and bread and potatoes joined the other foods already rationed. We did not find the measures as difficult as many others, for our previous circumstances had accustomed us to hardships. Shortly before our arrival in England the first snows of the winter had begun to fall. It was to be the most ferocious winter of the century, but we children were delighted as, day after day, the snow continued to fall from leaden skies.

Our joys were complete when my father built us a double-sized snowman constructed using two dustbins full of compacted snow. For many weeks that old snowman with his protruding carrot nose stood guard on the front lawn, for the snow fell each day until the middle of March. Like the rest of the country, we also shivered when the bitter weather created a fuel crisis. Rivers had frozen over, so that coal supplies could no longer be easily transported; many roads also were blocked by ten-foot drifts of snow.

Mindful of my recent serious illness, my parents sought medical advice to try to discover the cause. Before long x-ray plates revealed the tell-tale evidence of scarring on the lungs, indicating that I had been suffering from tuberculosis, probably contracted in India. Clearly my health problems had not all been imaginary. 'Your child could well experience related complications all her life', the consultant informed my dismayed parents. However, regular visits to a tuberculosis clinic, coupled with care and better food, had a beneficial effect, and the family had little cause for anxiety.

The year passed quickly. Visits to relatives gave the family opportunities of renewing bonds that had been severed for seven long years. For Stanley, and for Norah to a lesser degree, there was an exhausting round of deputation work to be undertaken. Eager supporters of the missionary society wished to meet them and to hear of the progress of the work to which they had dedicated their lives. Soon it was Christmas, and the delights of that season remained with me for years to come. Turning on his crackling old wireless set, my father told us that Santa's plane was almost overhead. Rushing upstairs he let down a sack of presents from the bedroom window on a rope. As the sack passed the sitting room window and landed with a thump in the garden, the excitement of the family knew no bounds, even though we older two strongly suspected that the story might be fictitious!

By the early summer of 1948 the time had come to return to China. Not only did Norah and Stanley face long separations from their children during their years of missionary service, but both also had ageing parents whom they might never see again. Stanley's father had died in 1936, the year that Christopher was born, and so had never seen his grandchildren at all. Stanley's mother had now reached the age of seventy-nine, but she was far from strong. Norah's father, who previously had an upright military bearing, seemed increasingly infirm, while her mother, now seventy-two years of age, bright and earnest in her Christian profession, found the long separations from her only daughter hard to bear. A family photograph was taken in London on the eve of our departure – a gift for the loved ones we must leave behind. With farewells at last completed the family embarked once more on another long voyage, this time by way of the Suez Canal, back to the Far East.

June 1948: Stanley and Norah;
Christopher, aged 12; Faith, aged 10; Philip, nearly 4.

8

AT SCHOOL IN THE MOUNTAINS

On our return to China in the summer of 1948 we found a country once more facing political turmoil. Since its inception in 1921, the Chinese Communist Party had been steadily gaining strength. The discontent, neglect, and exploitation of the peasant population, then almost eighty percent of the country, together with the corruption rife throughout the Chiang Kai-shek regime, had helped the Party to consolidate its hold on the heart of the nation. There had been a temporary coalition between Chiang Kai-shek's Nationalist forces and the Red Army for the period of the Japanese invasion, but with the withdrawal of the Japanese in 1945, civil war had broken out again, and there had been a race between the contending armies to occupy the liberated territories – a race largely won by the Communists. Spiralling inflation, food shortages, homelessness – all problems the Nationalist government had been slow to address – played into the hands of the Communist Party, and now, even to a casual observer, the progress of its advance seemed unstoppable.

What the consequences of these things would be, the missionaries did not know. But for the time being Stanley was anxious to return to his distant north-west mission station and to take up his work again while opportunity remained. A short spell in Shanghai at the mission headquarters was followed by the familiar separations. Christopher was now twelve and I was still ten years of age. Philip had recently turned four. For missionary parents, as well as for their children, the bleakness of these partings was painful. To Stanley and Norah it demonstrated the cost they were prepared to pay in their service to Christ for the sake of the Chinese people. For them it was the experience of the desolation, the aching loneliness of an empty and strangely silent home, and their uncertainty regarding their children's welfare. For us it was the bewilderment of loss, homesickness, and the impersonal demands of institutional life.

The school to which Christopher and I were now returning was in Guling (Kuling), in the province of Jiangsi (Kiangsi), one of China's most picturesque beauty spots, high up in the mountains. A nine-mile climb, culminating in one thousand steps hewn out of the mountainside, was a test of stamina which had to be undertaken in easy stages with many rests. Coolies carried the luggage slung from poles across their shoulders, and when young feet grew too tired to take another step, there might be the welcome respite of a ride in a sedan chair. Here in this mountain retreat, some 5,000 feet above sea level, the school was now catering for more than a hundred and thirty children aged six and upwards, in buildings sold to the China Inland Mission for the nominal sum of one dollar in gold.

In the surrounding countryside streams flowed freely along boulder-strewn river beds before tumbling in waterfalls into deep green pools. Tiger lilies grew wild on the mountainside, in random natural beauty. With a growing appreciation of

Tiger lilies growing wild

nature, I loved to roam the hillside, stopping to admire the exquisite loveliness of the pure white flowers with their angry red spots, or to sit quietly beside some stream watching the play of sun on water.

Long walks took the children to areas where they could view the rocky mountain crags known as Lion's Leap, or gaze up at the ancient splendour of the Three Trees – spectacular redwood evergreens towering high into the sky. Sometimes we visited the Three Graces – a deep foaming pool where three waterfalls threw their shiny cascades down from the height above. Here the braver swimmers could laugh and play, ducking each other under the waterfalls. Only the Emerald Grotto further down river with its silent green depths was considered dangerous. Each week the children would visit the swimming pool in the nearby town. I soon learned to swim and gained the necessary qualifications to venture into the 'deep end' where the water sunk to a phenomenal depth of twenty-five feet.

Winter held its unique pleasures. Heavy falls of snow brought the delight of riding on a toboggan packed with other young passengers as it raced down a steep track perhaps

Lion's Leap

The Three Trees

The Three Graces

three hundred feet in length. When the path ended abruptly at the verge of a sheer drop of six feet or more, the toboggan had reached so great a speed that it sailed high into the air, landing far out on the school playing-fields below. It would then shoot across the field before slowing to a standstill, allowing the laughing riders to tumble off in safety.

Extra-school facilities were arranged and I eagerly joined the Girl Guides. Here we were allocated to different patrols, learned the rudiments of knot tying, building camp fires and all the other skills necessary for survival in the wild. Uniforms were provided and each girl awarded a shining trefoil badge. I regarded mine with enormous pride. We learnt to cook a simple stew and enjoyed singing songs around the camp fire. Regular hikes were arranged, with the invariable picnic when we arrived at our destination.

With a continuing love of books, I now had the opportunity to discover a wider range of literature. As before, I would often memorize long passages that appealed to me. Kenneth Grahame's *Wind in the Willows* was a favourite, and I found myself intrigued and stirred by his descriptive language, but the chapter entitled *The Piper at the Gates of Dawn* touched me deeply. Something of the awesome majesty of the Divine, described by Grahame through the eyes of his animal characters, gripped me and I committed favourite sections to memory. Another writer whose artless tales fascinated me was Enid Blyton; but her books were considered unsuitable, and I was prohibited from reading them. Prohibition increases desire, and one day I discovered that copies of the forbidden books were kept in the Sick Bay, as the Infirmary was called, so that children there could while away the long hours. Surreptitiously I would creep along the dark passages, snatch the next book in the series, perhaps further exploits of *The Famous Five*, and read it in secret, before returning for a further volume when that was finished.

Medical care was excellent, and here Dr Robert Pearce and his wife Nellie reigned supreme. The doctor's interest in eye care was legendary, and most of the children were fitted up with a pair of spectacles before schooldays were done. I found myself confined to bed in the Sick Bay for several lengthy periods as the effect of tuberculosis still took its toll. My parents had packed the x-ray plates in the top of my school trunk, and each illness I had, however minor, was now treated seriously. Homesickness always seemed more acute at such times, and almost two years would pass, years of growing from a child to an adolescent, before I would see my parents again. Regular letters now passed between us although only one has survived – one that included an added note for my brother, Philip. In my imagination, however, my parents had taken on surreal characteristics. In an essay I had written entitled 'My Mother', the description of the fair curly-headed young woman of my imagination suggested that I would scarcely have recognized my real mother if I had met her unexpectedly.

In an attempt to compensate the younger boarders for the loss of individual attention, the school instituted a system of 'big brothers' and 'big sisters'. Each young child was paired with an older boy or girl, whose responsibility it was to act as any older brother or sister might towards a younger sibling – and many of the new boarders were little more than six years of age. Such a humane arrangement was indeed a comfort to homesick children, and a number kept in contact with their appointed 'brother' or 'sister' long after school days were over. As a ten-year-old, I was still considered young enough to benefit from such a system, and related well to the kindly older boarder, one of the doctor's daughters, who had been appointed for me. These years in Guling were therefore a much happier period of childhood. Yet even so, the loss of affection that only parents could provide often led to a certain desolation of spirit.

A Chinese tutor came regularly to the school to teach us written Chinese, but with her limited English, she found discipline hard to maintain, and we learnt little. Untidy and careless, I was still frequently in trouble; but now, with a settled and relaxed staff, punishments were more measured and appropriate. When I was caught flashing a small mirror in the sunlight so that the beam shone directly in the teacher's eyes, I was given a verse from the Psalms to write out many times over, 'Be not as the horse or as the mule which have no understanding' – a just retribution I did not quickly forget.

The genial influence of the headmaster, Stanley Houghton, and his kindly wife, whose own two teenage daughters were among the pupils, generated a relaxed and friendly atmosphere throughout the school. Their commitment to the welfare of the children was genuine and sacrificial. But a sad day came – a day few of the children will ever forget – when our headmaster suffered a fatal heart attack whilst playing a game of tennis with other members of the staff. At school prayers that very morning he had read to us from the Book of Deuteronomy, 'The beloved of the LORD shall dwell in safety by him' (*Deut.* 33:12). And now our headmaster had been taken to that place of safety. Grief and shock were palpable among pupils and staff alike. One member of staff pinned a poem on the school notice board; I read it and found the words expressed my own high esteem of Stanley Houghton:

> There were thorns and briars in the path he trod,
> He heeded not: he walked with God.
> He passed through rivers – he passed dry-shod,
> All unafraid: walking with God.

Meanwhile the Communist Party had continued to make steady advances and in November 1948, shortly after Stanley and Norah had returned to the country, Beijing had fallen. As the post-war capital, its fall was of vital psychological significance, and soon other cities followed like a pack of cards. Lanzhou, city of my birth, fell in August 1949. It was therefore no surprise to Stanley and Norah, nor to any watching the political map unfolding, when the Nationalist government suddenly collapsed as Mao Tse-tung, standing at the giant Gate of Heavenly Peace in Tienanmen Square, Beijing, gateway to the Forbidden City, proclaimed the People's Republic of China on 1 October 1949. Chiang Kai-shek, head of the Nationalist government for the last thirty years, fled the country, sailing to Taiwan in a cruiser said to be laden with all the gold bullion from the Bank of China! Now the iron grip of Communism, with its reforming agenda, was felt right across that vast land.

Throughout 1950 the People's Republic of China, or the CCP (Chinese Communist Party), as it became known, continued to tighten its hold on power. No one now knew who could be trusted. The Party had eyes and ears every-where, and even the most innocuous actions could be misconstrued as an offence against the new regime and lead to betrayal, torture and imprisonment. The American owner of a prestigious hotel in Guling, known as Fairy Glen, complete with seventy-eight rooms, and a number of bungalows in its two acres of ground, decided he could stand the strain no longer. He donated the Fairy Glen complex to the China Inland Mission for their use when missionaries came to visit their children, and left the country.

By July 1950, after my brother and I had been in Guling for two years, our parents decided they must attempt the long cross-country journey once more, a distance of some 1,750 miles, to bring Philip, recently turned six years of age, to boarding school for the first time. Travel permits had become increasingly hard to obtain, particularly for non-Chinese, unless of course they wished to leave the country. But Norah and Stanley succeeded in their application for a permit, and towards the end of July they arrived in Guling.

I was delighted to see my parents again, and even more so when I learnt that they planned to stay a number of weeks at Fairy Glen in order to spend as much time as possible with us. Even though I had missed my mother sorely, as a young adolescent I now experienced a strangeness, even awkwardness, in all my relationships with her. Conscious of physical changes as I moved towards teenage years, I avoided being alone with her at all costs. If ever we were left in a room together or even found ourselves walking side by side along a path, I discovered an inward panic developing and devised excuses to escape such a circumstance – a situation that must have been most hurtful for my mother. But in my relationship with my father, I had no such inhibitions. Alike in many ways, we knew an unusual compatibility of thought.

The weeks passed quickly and soon the time came when Stanley and Norah must leave us once more, to return to a home now empty and quiet.

Philip felt the parting acutely. Usually cheerful and confident he appeared lost and troubled. I had always felt a warmth of affection towards my young brother and now decided that he was my responsibility. I would always be there, I determined, as a representative of his home and a refuge if he should be in trouble. One of his teachers later recalled the child's affectionate nature, and treasured a seemingly insignificant gift she had once received from him. Mounted on a page in her diary she had glued a small nut-coloured leaf, and written, 'Little Philip pushed this tiny leaf into my hand, saying "Would you like this little leaf? It's a sort of moon shape."'

Faith aged 12 at Guling   Philip starting school, aged 6

Even as my parents left us in early September 1950 they
experienced a gnawing and growing fear: how long would the
school be able to function? How long before all missionaries
would be expelled from the country? With the CCP's in-built
antipathy to 'imperialist' influence and to any religious
affiliations, it could only be a matter of time before all
Christian missionaries were expelled from the country.
Christian institutions were being taken over one by one
during 1950: hospitals, colleges, schools and orphanages.
Christian broadcasting stations were ordered to close. The
government demanded the deeds of all foreign-owned
property in the country. In May of that year, at the summons
of Chou En-lai, a group of church leaders promised to co-
operate with the government and agreed to purge themselves
and their churches of any 'imperialist' influences. The
sacrificial care demonstrated by missionary societies to the
desperate needs of the people under Japanese occupation
seemed to have been quite forgotten, or were of little account
in this time of crisis.

Restrictions on the freedom that the Guling school was allowed were now tightening. Even as children, we became aware of the deteriorating situation. My photograph album with its treasured collection of pictures of the beauty spots around the school was confiscated. Surely, thought one misguided official, this album is being prepared for espionage work, and so he ripped out all but the few photographs shown earlier in this chapter before handing back the offending album. The children were forbidden to speak to any Chinese national: unguarded words could so easily be twisted and reported to the authorities, bringing serious repercussions on the missionary school.

Already Chinese Christians were under mounting pressure to compromise their faith. Their contact with the 'imperialist' missionaries made them vulnerable to a frightening degree of intimidation and even torture. And if the new government treated its own people like this, what would happen to foreign nationals? What if missionary families were split up? What if they, too, were imprisoned or tortured? Stanley and Norah did not know. The new government had not yet ordered the missionaries to leave the country, but their presence was clearly unwelcome and an increasing embarrassment to the Chinese Churches.

Scarcely had Stanley and Norah reached Pingluo once more before a message came from the mission headquarters that all missionaries were being advised to leave the country. The school in Guling was to be disbanded and parents should contact the school to check up on arrangements for collecting their children as soon as possible. It was a sad day indeed in the history of the China Inland Mission, which had laboured in that country for the last eighty-five years. Before the school disbanded all the children were required to destroy their treasured collections of letters from their parents, lest any comments written by parents to their children should fall into government hands, with possible severe repercussions for the parents. To destroy letters lovingly written and eagerly received was hard indeed for the missionaries' children.

Once more my brother Christopher and I would be involved in a flight from imminent danger; first it had been from Japanese forces and now from a determined and atheistic Communist government. The immediate imperative for the school was to evacuate the buildings and to check that all travel arrangements for the children were satisfactory.

Whatever might ensue, at least the families must not be broken apart. Gradually the school began to disperse. For Christopher, Philip, and me this meant a long, and potentially dangerous journey across China – eventful at any time but more so given the political circumstances, and the fact that it was to be undertaken during the coldest months of the year.

9

INTO THE UNKNOWN

Starting out in November 1950, we travelled under the supervision of the staff, together with a group of others whose parents lived in the same general direction, a journey of some seven hundred miles, undertaken mainly by train. Meanwhile my father came as far as Xi-an in the province of Shaanxi where it was arranged that he should pick up his children and take us the rest of the way himself, another thousand miles or more, to the north-western town of Pingluo. This journey was to be undertaken largely in open lorries, with the family perched high up among the goods the vehicle might be carrying. Only Philip, as youngest in the party, had the privilege of travelling in the cab with the driver, but for Christopher and me there was no respite from the intense cold as temperatures plummeted far below freezing. Long hours were spent trundling along roads deeply rutted by the wheels of carts. The only breaks in the day occurred at the convenience of the driver, not at the request of any member of the chilled family bumping along among the goods on top of the vehicle.

As darkness fell, the driver would seek the nearest inn in some remote village along the way. Sometimes the family was privileged with a *k'ang* for the night. This mud-baked platform-bed filled half the allotted space in the room, and underneath it a fire was stoked up that burned slowly all night, warming up the mud bed – a primitive sort of electric blanket! The windows of the room were mere framed holes, protected from the elements by nothing but paper, while a padded cloth hung across the aperture that acted as a doorway. Fleas and bedbugs abounded in this primitive accommodation, mercifully hidden from our view by the dim lighting – a sputtering oil lamp that rested in an alcove in the wall, casting strange shadows around the room. With no possibility of undressing at night, nor even the provision of washing facilities apart from a bowl of water, all four members of the family rolled up thankfully together on matting on top of the *k'ang*, with a loose covering thrown over us. Hard as the bed was, sleep soon came to the weary travellers. Often the smouldering fuel from the *k'ang* fire belched out fumes into the room, which the sleepers inhaled all night. This led to an easily recognisable headache known in Chinese as *shuinla* – a condition that would often persist all the following day.

Toilet facilities were primitive in the extreme. As in Tianshui, each inn provided a large cesspit dug at the end of the inn yard. Across this pit two planks, often filthy and slippery, were cast. The stench was appalling, and the danger of falling in a reality. I had seen the pathetic remains of animals that had met their end in such circumstances, not to mention the ever-present rats scurrying around. On one occasion I needed to cross the yard in the middle of the night. Worming my way carefully out of the communal *k'ang* bed, I struggled across the yard avoiding ice-covered potholes, in order to find the public pit in the dark and cold. As I started to return to the inn room my presence alerted the geese, whose activities as alarm raisers filled a useful function for the inn keeper. Trembling and panic-stricken I fled stumblingly back across the open yard with a flock of hissing geese in hot pursuit – a venture I sincerely hoped might never be repeated.

Sometimes 'there was no room in the inn'. Where could we sleep? Accommodation would eventually be found in some local hall furnished with narrow backless benches. Balancing on such a bench through the night proved an uncomfortable and uncertain experience, and the chance of rolling off onto the hard mud floor was very high. However, toughened by all I had endured, this sometimes proved a more acceptable, though colder, option than the *k'angs* provided by the inns.

When no lorry driver could be found who was willing to take the English family in the direction in which they wished to travel, Stanley would engage the services of some cart driver eager for a little extra pay. Tediously the hours passed by as the mule team dragged the rickety cart along the rough tracks. At last however the travel-worn family reached Lanzhou, the largest city before Ningxia. Normally we might have rested for a few days at the Borden Memorial Hospital, but the previous year it had been annexed by the new government and most of the mission staff had been evacuated. Only one person remained – it was Stanley and Norah's doctor friend, who had cared for Norah when she suffered from septicaemia after Godfrey's birth. Dr Rupert Clarke was under arrest, accused of manslaughter because he had been unable to restore a dying man to health.

Before we reached Pingluo the Huang Ho would have to be crossed. Gone were all the turbulent waters at this time of year and instead the river was transformed into a sheet of solid ice, ten feet or more thick. So strong was the ice that lorries could drive straight across with no fear that it would break under their weight. The mule drawn cart in which our family had been travelling would also have to cross in the same way. But hooves shod with metal were by no means as secure as rubber tyres. As the animals slithered and skidded on the ice, it became imperative to lighten their load, and we all jumped down, delighted to make our own way on foot across the icy river.

At last, with the final lap of that long and arduous journey completed, we were glad to arrive at our own mission station in Pingluo. Hung over the doorway of the living accommodation was a large banner with the single word 'Welcome' emblazoned in bright red letters, prepared by Norah to celebrate her home-coming family.

The joy of a family Christmas was muted by the impending sense of crisis. Stanley knew it could only be a matter of weeks before he would be forced to leave his missionary labours. He was anxious, therefore, to use every moment he could spare for preaching and teaching the people. Who would instruct them when he was gone? Many were weak Christians. Would they be able to withstand the onslaught on their faith by an all-powerful government determined to destroy all forms of religious faith among its people?

Early in the new year Stanley was prohibited from leaving the town without express permission from the local Communist bureaucracy. At once this severely curtailed his missionary activity. No longer could he cycle out to the surrounding villages, preach in their market places and distribute tracts. Nevertheless he gave his time to evangelistic activity still open to him. I found that my

Chinese, little used since the age of six, soon began to come back to me. I was able to follow much conversation, understand a sermon and even communicate cheerfully with the local people, much as I had done as a small child.

Temperatures fell to a bitter 40°C below freezing. Clad in a padded Chinese gown over my own normal clothes, I still felt the barbed icy arrows penetrating all defences. Even the moisture in my long plaited hair seemed to freeze overnight and with hands paralysed by cold in the morning I could not begin to undo my plaits in order to tidy my hair each day. We children would watch in amazement as drops of hot tea falling on the table froze to solid lumps before our eyes.

One pleasure, however, brought me much delight. I was given a puppy for Christmas – a strange gift in view of the uncertainty surrounding our future. White, with irregular patches of brown, the good-natured pup and I became inseparable. The warmth of his little body unfroze my hands, and the devotion of the small creature became a constant source of comfort. *Mebor*, which means 'fat and self-satisfied' in Chinese, was the name I gave to my pet and *Mebor* enjoyed privileges that would shock most self-respecting animal owners. He was allowed to share my bed at night. A canine hot-water bottle, he only surfaced when he felt the need of air and then transformed himself into a living pulsating scarf around my neck.

But even I realised that at any time I would be parted from my pet, and indeed from the country of my birth, as an order for our expulsion appeared imminent. And early in March 1951 we found ourselves under house arrest. Slowly the restrictions on Stanley's movements had been increasing. But this last step spelled the end. With every avenue of Christian service closed to him, the veteran missionary prepared to leave China – the land of his adoption – and without delay. Then came the ultimatum. A deadline was given by which he and our family must be out of the house. The results of disobedience were unspecified, but not difficult to guess.

Frantic days followed as we packed up as many belongings as we could carry. Philip was excited at the prospect of another journey to England; Christopher was silent, and I grief-stricken at the thought of parting with *Mebor*. On the appointed day the local Party representatives punctually arrived to oversee the departure. As each room was vacated a sheet of paper was glued across the doorway to make sure that no one could return. We children were carefully frisked from head to foot to check we were not carrying hidden weapons or other stolen goods. Clambering on to the waiting lorry, Stanley and Norah took a last long look at their home, the scene of many labours and sacrifice, before the vehicle rumbled off amid a shower of dust and gradually gathered speed, our immediate destination now Hong Kong, more than a thousand miles distant as the crow flies.[1]

With rising temperatures, as winter gave place to spring, the journey to the coast was less arduous than the long inland trek. As we reached central China we were able to travel by train for much of the remaining distance. Instead of First Class or Second Class travel, Chinese trains of the time only provided Soft Seats or Hard Seats – and for the Rowe family it was Hard Seats. These were basic wooden benches in long carriages which soon became overcrowded to the point of

[1] According to a conservative estimate in 1994 by Amity News Service, there were 1,800 baptized believers in the Pingluo churches (see Tony Lambert, *China's Christian Millions*, Monarch Books/OMF International, 1999, p. 230). In later years it was a great joy to Stanley to receive many letters from those who first heard the gospel from him.

suffocation. As the train pulled into a station, hungry passengers piled out to try to buy a little food before the train chugged off down the line once more, often with extra passengers clinging to the outer doors of the train or even scrambling up on to the roof. After several weeks the exhausted family eventually arrived in Canton, the last town before we crossed into British held Hong Kong. Here we found excellent accommodation and enjoyed a few days respite, exploring the tree-lined streets, resting in the dappled shade and subsisting largely on a diet of bananas which were plentiful and cheap. At last came the long hot day when we queued to pass through the border customs into free Hong Kong. There in the distance, just across the border, fluttered the British flag – symbol of liberty – which I would remember long afterwards, together with the surge of relief and joy that the sight engendered.

Accommodation would be impossible to find in Hong Kong, so the mission had been informed when it first began to make preparations for the mass withdrawal of its seven hundred or more personnel. Seriously overcrowded even under normal circumstances, the colony was facing an acute problem in trying to provide for the influx of escapees from the hostile Communist regime – men, women and children who could only be described as refugees.

But not long before our arrival, a semi-dismantled and derelict army camp down by the sea, complete with eleven Nissan huts with rusting corrugated roofs, had been placed at the disposal of the China Inland Mission. Not only had this provision been made, but finance too was to hand to renovate the property. In a surprising gesture, the Communist officials in Shanghai had offered the Mission three years advance rent for the use of its two multi-storied buildings in

Sinza Road. This was the more amazing because the normal policy had been simply to commandeer foreign property without offering any compensation. Surely this was a token of God's providence and care at so distressing a time in the history of the China Inland Mission.

Quickly arranging for the restoration of water and electricity, the mission purchased two hundred and fifty camp beds and six hundred blankets. To these Nissan huts, with their basic but adequate provision, our travel-weary family was directed and here we would be housed while awaiting a flight back to England. Of necessity families were split up, men and women being accommodated separately. I discovered a bed allocated to me – one of a long line of beds – among women young and old, all entire strangers to me.

The sights and sounds of Hong Kong shocked and surprised me. As a sensitive teenager, unaccustomed to a western-style lack of modesty, I found the brash advertising blazing from shop fronts offensive. Unsettled, and filled with teenage self-consciousness, I reacted badly to my circumstances, proving less than helpful to my parents, whose own lives had also been so radically torn apart. Not many weeks passed, however, before a Dakota aeroplane became available and was chartered to take the first contingent of missionaries and children, thirty adults and sixteen children in all, together with other foreign nationals, back to Britain.

Clambering up the flight steps into the waiting aircraft, I found a seat next to my father, which pleased me. Scarcely had the plane left the ground, however, before I grabbed a bag thoughtfully provided for travel sick passengers. As the air hostess came past to check that everyone had settled in, Stanley called out jovially, 'Six bags for this young lady, please.' He spoke truer than he knew. The entire journey took four days, and as the Dakota plunged and rose in pockets of air, I was unable to stop being sick. With exceptional consideration the pilot pointed out significant locations as we flew over them, especially the countries of the Middle East, and Israel in particular, which he thought would be of interest to his passengers. But I was quite unable to benefit from such an experience.

Each night the plane landed at some airport and the weary travellers were conducted to a local hotel. From my jaundiced perspective I noted that we were required to sleep in sheets that had not been changed since their previous user had occupied the bed. It seems I had forgotten, at least temporarily, that not many months ago I had slept balanced on a narrow bench. Even at night I had no relief from the cycle of sickness.

At last the plane circled over Hertfordshire, flying into a small airport near Bovingdon. The party alighted slowly and thankfully from the Dakota, but as we stepped on to the tarmac on a cool English April day, we were astonished to find press reporters waiting to greet us.

All sixteen children were grouped together for a photograph, and the next day the *News Chronicle* – a broad-sheet long since absorbed by another paper – carried the headline 'Smiling children – and all from China'. Yes, I was smiling in the photograph, but it was a forced smile. Christopher belied the headline with a scowl, probably annoyed by a crying baby not far from him, while six-year-old Philip's smile was only an apprehensive one at best. Under the caption were words spoken by one of the party, 'Christian missionaries in China are slowly being compelled to withdraw. We still have about 300 men and women and 100 children out there.'

SMILING CHILDREN—AND ALL FROM CHINA

SIXTEEN children—all but one of them in the picture flew in to Bovingdon, Hertfordshire, from Hong Kong yesterday.

With 30 men and women, they had begun a mass withdrawal, ordered by the China Inland Mission, of Protestant missionaries and their families from China.

"Christian missionaries in China are slowly being compelled to withdraw," said an official. "We still have about 300 men and women and 100 children out there."

★

Linguist among the children was eight-year-old Kenneth Grant (extreme left), of Alberta, Canada. He learned Chinese from friends in Kunming, Yunnan Province, where his father served.

"Ngo chin tien tso fei chi" (I came by plane), he said.— News Chronicle picture.

March/April '51

Cutting from the *News Chronicle*

From the airport the party was driven to the mission headquarters in north London. Let loose amid unending corridors, each with individual bedrooms, we children soon regained our spirits and enjoyed running and chasing each other from landing to landing, doubtless without due regard to elderly residents. I had always felt a particular affinity with my young brother Philip, and so passed my time teaching him to read.

Never again would we revisit the land of our birth: even our grasp of the Chinese language would soon dwindle to a few scattered phrases. Although as children we gradually came to understand that it was love to Christ, love to the Chinese peoples, and a strong sense of Christian duty, that had motivated our parents, the sacrifices and loss of home life since the age of six had undoubtedly been a heavy burden to bear – not only for us but also for many other children of missionary parents.

10

TWO PINK SUGAR MICE

It was late April and my parents faced the pressing problem of finding suitable schools for us. Clarendon School, a Christian boarding school for girls, situated in North Wales, kindly offered places to a number of the party even though extra beds had to be purchased to accommodate the girls in a school already filled to capacity. With no time even for the purchase of school uniform, I soon found myself on a train bound for North Wales.

The whole family came to the station to see me off, and a lasting memory was the sight of fair-haired Philip waving frantically as the train slowly gathered speed. His affection meant much to me and the thought of not seeing him for several months saddened me. Accommodation was arranged for the rest of the family in Cliftonville, a suburb of Margate on the south-east coast. Here Stanley and Norah would set up home for my brothers who would both be attending local schools.

The summer term had already started by the time we arrived, but from the very first I loved my new school. After all I had experienced it seemed a haven of happiness. The imposing building with its square forecourt, grand entrance hall, mysterious-looking turrets and towers, appealed to my imagination. The grounds, with their wide paths, tall trees, impressive rhododendron bushes and surrounding parkland provided the pupils with ideal surroundings. New-born lambs, staggering after their mothers or bleating helplessly when they could not find them, were a familiar enough sight for most of the girls, but for me it was all new. The larch woods at the edge of the grounds, clothed in their new growth of tender greens beckoned to me to come and explore, but I soon learnt that they were out of bounds. And the daffodils, almost over by the time the summer term began, provided another new delight. At the back of the school lay the formal Venetian Gardens, complete with an ornamental lily pond, but again I discovered that only the privileged senior girls were allowed to walk sedately among the shaped trees.

Hastily clothed from a box of second-hand uniform, we newcomers no longer stood out as distinct from the other boarders. I soon discovered, however, that I was seriously behind in many of my subjects and would have to work hard to reach the standard expected of the class. French and Latin

Grounds at Clarendon

Clarendon School – rear view

proved problematic because all the others had already covered the foundation work and I had not touched these subjects. But with wise and sympathetic encouragement I began to make progress. Unused to the dignified conduct expected of the daughters of the well-to-do, I once again found myself in many scrapes. To scramble out of the high windows and climb gingerly along the turrets and chimney pots on the roof was a particular challenge to my venturesome spirit. Perhaps there were secret passage ways waiting to be discovered, I thought, with a mind still crammed full of the exploits of Enid Blyton's characters. I would soon learn that such conduct carried serious consequences.

With little idea of the decorum expected at such a school as Clarendon, I posed constant problems for the school matron. Beds had to be aired in a regulated way every morning, with each blanket stripped off and folded into three. Routines of this nature were not easy for a thirteen-year-old straight from rat-infested inland China with little training in such exacting protocol. The usual punishment for offending boarders was to be sent to the matron's bathroom to await her arrival. Many were the times I found myself standing in the small bathroom studying the details of that lady's personal possessions, until she herself arrived to administer

Two Pink Sugar Mice

One corner of Miss Swain's drawing room

the necessary reproof. If the matron forgot that she had already sent one child to her bathroom, she might well send another, and another, until on occasions the bathroom could hold no more juvenile culprits.

Most of all I was in awe of Miss Swain, the headmistress. Tall, elderly and fragile-looking, she yet controlled her school with iron discipline. One raised finger could bring order to an unruly classroom of girls. Always accompanied by a large white deaf-aid which squeaked and screeched as she adjusted the volume, the headmistress carried with her an aura of quiet dignity. For one night each week an entire class was invited to her drawing room where the girls would sit and embroider or knit for an annual sale of work for some good cause, while Miss Swain read aloud from some account of missionary endeavour; or on occasions recited long poems to the girls who listened, astonished that any one brain could remember so much material at one time.

Any interview with Miss Swain was a daunting experience, particularly for a child who climbed on school roofs. One day towards the end of my first term, I received a message that the head wished to see me immediately in her private flat. Never had I ventured near these precincts before and, as I tiptoed down the wide gloomy corridor, I began to wonder wildly what I could have done so seriously wrong to merit a personal interview. Knocking timidly on her personal sitting room door, I heard a distant voice calling me to come in. With thumping heart I entered but at first could see no one. Then came a voice from the depths of a large floral upholstered chair. 'Sit down, my dear,' said Miss Swain, with a wave towards an empty chair. Her voice was kindly – a voice that betrayed some emotion. Puzzled, I sat down on the chair indicated. 'Do you trust in the Lord Jesus Christ?' was the startling question, put to me.

Although I had often thought on spiritual issues, had often found consolation in God in times of crisis or distress and had often prayed for forgiveness for my many sins, such thoughts as these were not prominent in my mind at that particular period of my life. Confronted with so bald a question, I scarcely knew what to say, but managed to stammer out, 'Yes, I do'. 'Well, you must trust him today as you have never done before,' continued the headmistress tenderly. Tears began to course down her old cheeks as she told me, as gently as she could, that my young brother Philip had been killed in a road accident. The austere headmistress and the bewildered child wept together, the one with genuine compassion for the tragedy that had befallen the missionary family, and the other in shock and distress.

As soon as I was able to listen, Miss Swain attempted to explain the circumstances of the accident. A confident young cyclist, Philip had been riding to some local swimming baths, accompanied by my mother. My older brother, Christopher, had gone on ahead. Emerging from their own road, Philip had announced, 'This is where we ring our bells, Mummy.' The next junction led on to a major road, a bus route. Again the boy and his mother stopped and watched until the road was clear from one direction; but then quite unaccountably,

Philip, who had just turned seven years of age, shot right across the road without checking to see if any traffic was approaching from the other direction. He rode straight into the path of a double-decker bus. Neither he nor the bus driver stood any chance of avoiding the collision. Philip was killed instantly. Norah, who was actually spared the anguish of witnessing the accident, presumed that the child had crossed in safety. Not until moments later as she joined the small crowd of passengers who had spilled out on to the pavement did she realize that it was her son caught under the wheels of that bus. July 14, 1951, is a date I will never forget.

The news cut to the very heart of my affection. I had loved Philip dearly and tried in my own way to mother my small brother. Such a loss would remain an acute wound for many years to come. But for the moment I was scarcely able to comprehend it. A kindly member of staff took me out for the rest of the day to the nearby town, but all I really wanted was to be alone, to try and grapple with my emotions. As I lay in bed that night, tossing and turning, half-asleep, half-awake, I became aware of a tall woman approaching my bed. Standing over me, the figure paused for a moment or two. Then she bent down, kissed me and slipped out. Was that my headmistress? I never knew, but from that time, despite all my misdemeanours, a bond of warm affection was established between us.

My father had just arrived at a conference in the Lake District at the time of the accident, but as soon as he received a telegram bearing the grievous news, he travelled all night to be back with my mother. A small funeral service was arranged for the following week, but strangely no suggestion was made that I should return home for the

Philip on his seventh birthday

occasion or be with my parents at such a time of grief, even though the term had only a few more days to run. Perhaps my parents felt it would be more than I could bear – perhaps they were reluctant for me to witness their sorrow – I never knew the reason for the omission, but always regretted that I had not been present. Bright and good-natured the boy had been loved by all who knew him and the words my parents chose for the gravestone were simple: 'With Christ – Lovely memories: glorious hope'.

A desolated family greeted me as I returned to Cliftonville. My mother was clearly in shock and my father silent in grief. Christopher appeared traumatised by the event. Was he blaming himself for the accident, because the outing had been undertaken at his request? I did not know. Certainly he was not to blame. More than fifty years later he can still remember the licence number of the bus that killed his brother. As my parents faced their loss with quiet courage, I learned a new respect for them. Norah had written to her own mother just a few hours after the accident: 'We do not sorrow as those who have no hope, for "it is well with the child". Only we suffer – nothing can ever hurt Philip again. Please pray that our laddie's going may bring glory to God's name.'

In later years, however, I came to see that such fortitude, though admirable, could also act as cloak for their sorrows and delay that inner healing through faith so needful to them. Never, either then or in the future, did my parents ever speak to me of our loss in a personal way or discuss the bereavement with me. In a sense it could be said that Norah's spirit suffered permanent damage through her grief. A triumphalist teaching, advanced by various 'holiness movements' that frowned on any admission of weakness, sin or spiritual failure, had produced an artificial and harmful stoicism among many Christians. Dr Martyn Lloyd-Jones, minister of Westminster Chapel, London, where both my parents now had their membership, touched on this very issue in a kindly letter he wrote to them:

> As we would expect from you, your letter is full of triumphant faith. But we are not meant to be unnatural, and you are bound to feel the loss and the absence of such a bright spirit very keenly. We can but assure you of our heart-felt sympathy and of our constant remembrance of you in our prayers. We know that God's ways are always perfect, and we must rest in and on that knowledge.

Perhaps the sight that distressed me personally more than anything else was to find among Philip's few small treasures two pink sugar mice – half eaten. Both heads were gone: all that remained were their rumps and long string tails. Numbed by the discovery and its wordless story of my loss, the sight became almost a symbol to me of a young life so suddenly and unexpectedly cut off. The question my headmistress had asked took on serious proportions for me, particularly when I also found among my brother's few possessions a dog-eared copy of the Gospel of John. In front was a childish picture of a windmill, but at the back in his large uncertain hand he had filled in his name under a printed but personal declaration of faith. Philip had been killed just two weeks after his seventh birthday. If so young a child could be snatched away in death without any warning, surely the question of my own personal standing with God was a matter I needed to address without delay.

A short family holiday followed at Ferring-on-Sea – a strained, silent and sad holiday without Philip's cheerful chatter. Unknown to me, my parents had already been planning an early return to the Far East, taking Philip with them. As all entry to China was denied, the mission had been exploring the possibility of evangelistic work in other south-east Asian countries: and now the 'new fields', as they became known, were beckoning. So Christopher and I faced a further shock: our parents now told us that despite Philip's death they would still be offering to return to the mission field as soon as possible. Christopher was to become a boarder at St Lawrence College in Ramsgate, a well-reputed public school, while I would continue my education at Clarendon.

Malaysia, where New Resettlement Villages presented a promising challenge to Christian missionaries, was to be their destination. These defensive sites, protected by fencing from the surrounding jungle, were established between 1948 and 1960, during the period known as the Emergency when the British administration was trying to prevent the communist guerrilla forces hiding deep in the jungle from preying on the local population. Stanley and Norah Rowe were the first couple to offer themselves for service in this new venture.

My father's commitment to his missionary work was all-consuming: at times it was almost obsessive in character. To be torn from it caused him mental anguish, a fact that may have blinded him to the needs of his two remaining teenaged children. A fresh separation from our parents so soon after Philip's death was little less than catastrophic for my brother and me. Bruised and grieving, we needed nothing more than a period of stable home life as an emotional healing. Was it right for the missionary society to accept my parents' services under such conditions? The idea that unknown people on the other side of the world had a greater need of Stanley and Norah's presence and devotion than their own two children at this traumatic time was surely misguided at best.

To understand such a decision, however, we must appreciate the ethos in which it was made. An immense value was placed upon this sort of sacrifice by the Christian community in general and it was viewed as honourable and highly commendable. An unrealistic heroism characterised many of these pioneers. 'I am glad,' said one noble veteran missionary, father of four small children, 'to have an alabaster box so precious to break at the Master's feet.' But if he had seen his six-year-old sobbing herself to sleep at night in the school dormitory, he might have wondered whether he had rightly understood the Saviour's injunction about leaving wife, children, houses and lands for his and the gospel's sake. These men and women felt they were offering up to their God their 'Isaacs' – their most valued possession – as indeed they were; but sadly, the question they did not address was whether God required such sacrifice. Were not their own children's souls also precious in the Saviour's sight? They could not have foreseen the lasting damage, mental and spiritual, suffered by many missionaries' children who grew up feeling they had been forsaken by their parents in the years when they needed them most.

The China Inland Mission was by no means alone in the emphasis that regarded family responsibilities as secondary to the call of God. The same confusion of priorities was to be found across the entire spectrum of missionary service and of Christian work as a whole, with many children sent to boarding school to free the parents for Christian endeavour. However mistaken the decision to leave their two older children at so vulnerable a time in our lives may have been, there can be no doubting my parents' desire above all to please and serve their God. Nor were they hard-hearted or insensitive to our needs. Far from it – the personal cost for them was high, in fact it almost amounted to a second bereavement. In days when the pendulum has swung to the opposite extreme so that duty has become a cinderella – and sacrifice for Christ's sake a rare commodity – it may well be easy to point the finger of blame, but harder to find equal devotion.

In spite of the undeniable emotional deprivation suffered by the children of the missionaries, many of us have also been thankful to God for the heritage of prayer and dedication bequeathed to us both by our parents and by the missionary societies that supported them. Today with cheap airfares and ease of communication, the situation for missionary families is far different, but in the early 1950s the problem of divided loyalties and mistaken priorities was acute and distressing, and one that was not adequately addressed.

11

POSTAL PARENTS

A passage on the P & O *Carthage* was booked for Stanley and Norah in early January 1952, only eight months after our family had first arrived back from China. It was a subdued Christmas we spent together that year, the last for some years to come. Frantic packing followed, purchasing school uniform and preparing for the long outward journey back to the Far East, this time by sea. A round of speaking engagements filled the days for my parents and seemingly eased the ache of the forthcoming separation. As the day of parting drew ever nearer, I noticed a new tenderness in their attitude towards me – a tenderness that only added to my distress. And at last came the day of departure. It would be four years before we would see them again. Photographs were taken on the steps of the mission headquarters, as all joined to wish the departing missionaries well. Norah's expression told a story, as did fifteen-year-old Christopher's forced smile, for in reality, the boy's spirit was at breaking point.

On we went to the station where our parents would board a train to Southampton. A large contingent of missionary personnel followed, for this departure was highly significant for the entire future of the mission, urgently seeking a new role for its operations now the door to China was closed. I found myself thrust to the back of the crowd as the train slowly moved off. Suddenly one more thoughtful friend spotted the irony of the situation and pushed me to the front to catch the last glimpse of my parents as they stood waving at the window of the train, my mother looking tense and tearful, and my father strained.

Back at the mission home once more, we were at a loose end. No guardian had yet been appointed to care for us, although one or two kindly adults helped out if I asked for assistance. The Spring term would soon begin and I was glad. Some of my new clothes were too long and needed altering, and I discovered with alarm that the shoe repairer considered my school shoes beyond his skills to patch up. Never handy with a needle, I tried my best to turn up the hems myself. At last the third week of January arrived and I was on the train back to my well-loved school – a place I now regarded as home.

Although soon immersed once more in all the trivia of boarding school life, I found time each week to write a letter to my parents. The first few letters were addressed to ports en route for Malaysia where the P & O *Carthage* would call: Aden, Penang and then to Singapore to await their arrival. Stanley and Norah treasured these schoolgirl epistles, storing them all up, until at last my father would present his married daughter with a shoe box crammed with letters dating from January 1952 until the time that he and my mother finally retired from missionary service in Malaysia more than twenty years later. These letters form a unique commentary on the development of a postal relationship with my parents that would form the bedrock of my security and development from a young teenager to womanhood and beyond. Faithfully my parents replied to each letter, commenting on my progress, chiding when they could sense my behaviour was becoming erratic, and offering advice as well as they were able.

Not long after arriving back at the mission headquarters in London at the end of the spring school term, I discovered that a middle-aged couple had been appointed as guardians for the children of the missionaries: Louis and Nancy Gaussen. Understanding and kindly, they were well-suited to care for the children. 'Mr and Mrs Gaussen are very nice,' I reported to my parents, 'but they'll never make up for not having you here in England.' Christopher and I were the first two of the many who would ultimately benefit from the care of this devoted couple. As no accommodation was yet available for a children's home, the mission headquarters with its endless long corridors and exciting, if gloomy, boxrooms remained my home for the time being.

The search for permanent premises for a hostel continued, but, with the approach of the summer school holidays, it was decided that the best plan was to use the mission's property, *The Chalet*, in Bidborough, Kent, as a temporary base. At the end of July 1952 my brother and I, together with two or three other young people, were taken there for the summer months. Because it was the very same house where we had spent a happy year together as a family in 1947, the place was full of memories for me. This made it no easier. I remembered the old snowman that my father had once made; it had stood on that same front lawn; there grew the same beech tree I had loved to climb – even the ornaments in the house were unchanged. But the sight of the eggcup shaped like a duck which Philip had always insisted on having for his boiled eggs brought back yet more poignant reminders of the brother I had lost. References to Philip can be found peppered throughout my correspondence with my parents: 'I often think of him,' I would write, 'I never realised how much I loved him and often long for opportunities to speak to him once more.'

Passing through the difficult teenage years, with in-built resentments against my situation, I was not an easy young person to handle, particularly as my guardians had had no previous experience of dealing with teenagers. But the love, patience and understanding shown by the couple towards the children in their care – motivated by a stronger love, a love to Christ – gradually conquered me. Before many months had passed a strong bond of affection had been established between us. Eventually a large suburban house with extensive gardens known as Maxwell House – formerly the home of some millionaire – in Chislehurst, Kent, was leased to the mission. By Christmas the home was ready and furnished and now twenty or more children were being cared for by Louis and Nancy Gaussen and their helpers during each school holiday.

I had found my school a place of happiness and friendship and, after an uncertain start, had accepted my situation in the children's hostel. Christopher, on the other hand, faced a challenge for which he was unprepared. Wounded from all his recent experiences, it was not easy for him to settle back into the patterns and strictures of boarding school life. Disturbed and distressed, especially by the events surrounding our brother Philip's death, his behaviour deteriorated. Before long it was decided that he should leave school soon after his sixteenth birthday. In the circumstances my parents offered to return and Stanley gave himself to urgent prayer for his son. But to bring his parents back from the mission field would only underline to Christopher the extremity of the situation and for this he was quite unwilling. Christopher now took a temporary job serving in a Lyons Tea Room, and tried to further his education by evening classes. The bond between us was strong; to me, he was the representative of my family; I championed his cause, grieving and worrying if he was in any trouble. As soon as he was eighteen he was liable for National Service and opted to join the Royal Navy. The regularity and strenuous discipline of navy life calmed and settled the young man. But it was a personal spiritual experience of God revealed in his Son Jesus Christ, that transformed him. Here he found not only forgiveness for all his past but motivation for living. Yet the scars remained, and Christopher would carry the marks of his early sufferings for many years.

Reading through some of these letters to my parents, I discover a graphic snapshot of typical boarding school life: friendships, examinations, sports, achievements, misconduct with its inevitable consequences . . . The protective environment – certainly over-protective for young people from secure home backgrounds – was exactly what I most needed to give me stability and equilibrium after all my chequered experiences. Since early childhood, my parents and later my teachers had given me careful and faithful Bible teaching. At times I had made a personal response of faith to all that I had been taught. Then a loss of interest suggested that it had only been a temporary concern, based on the felt needs of a moment. But slowly and certainly, over the next two years I gained a clear and unshakeable assurance of the mercy of God through Christ's sacrifice on my behalf. Like many children of Christian parents I can never date my conversion. Only, as one so often bereft of parental care, I now knew the love of One who had promised never to leave or forsake me.

Long rambles among Welsh beauty spots filled many weekends but these were also the times when I could feel most desolate in spirit since many weekly boarders went home. But there were compensations: one member of the housekeeping staff, whose own sister – a kindly person – had joined the staff of our school in India in 1946, took a special interest in me. As my birthday came round each year Pamela Harris prepared a beautifully decorated cake to celebrate the occasion. Miss Swain's sister, who together with her husband, Harold St John, well-loved leader among the Brethren, shared a flat in the school premises, often invited me to join her for a cup of tea – a privilege not extended to many of the boarders. The St John family, who well knew the experience of long family separations on account of missionary work, did all they could to ease the sense of loss I so often felt. Although my reckless daring still often led me into trouble, a number of the members of staff took a special interest in my progress and seemed to show unexpected affection towards me. And still I remained a firm favourite with the headmistress – a definite advantage.

Telephone links to the Far East were either not yet established at that time, or else prohibitively expensive. Such a means of contact, regarded as commonplace today, was therefore not available to my brother and me or to others whose parents were abroad. With remarkable compassion and insight, the Rev. Elsie Chamberlain of the BBC arranged for a group of young people in these circumstances to broadcast personal Christmas messages to their parents – an arrangement which would later be extended to a second broadcast during the summer. Each year a different group of young people would be chosen for the privilege; I was among the first to send a live message to the Far East in December

1953. The nervous thrill of travelling up to Broadcasting House to record my message was one that I will not easily forget.

Each week I continued to write to my parents and each week they replied. I poured out my affection in these letters, often heaping reassurances of my love upon them as I concluded each letter. Although I missed them sorely, the same triumphalist emphasis that governed evangelical Christians in general at the time had been carefully inculcated in the younger generation. I had been taught never to give any impression of unhappiness or loneliness when I wrote to my parents in case it brought them distress and acted as a hindrance to the work to which they were dedicated. The lesson was driven home on one particular occasion when I had asked Mrs Gaussen how to spell the word 'doleful'. When it came to light that I had actually used that word in one my letters, it became a cause of serious concern in the home and even a matter for special united prayer lest the use of the word should suggest that I was less than happy. In my next letter I earnestly apologised in case it had caused my parents any anxiety.

Time seemed to kaleidoscope in my mind as the months passed. In June 1954, after my parents had been away for two and a half years, I wrote anticipating their return as if it were imminent: 'I am sort of living in the future the whole time. You will come and see me when you come home, won't you? You probably won't recognise me at first . . .' In reality I had a further eighteen months to wait. Stanley and Norah, for their part, did all they could from a distance to ease the pain of separation. They sent parcels of clothes, urgently enquiring after their daughter's ever-changing measurements at any given time; frequently they stinted themselves to send a little extra pocket money to provide small luxuries which they would willingly have given had they been at home.

A bond of correspondence was built up over the years: I prayed for the people mentioned in their letters; family jokes were repeated and expanded from one week to the next. I was developing a degree of facility with my pen and many were the lively tales of my exploits with which I regaled my bemused parents, often adding small stick illustrations to enhance the effect. The day that my friends and I decided to scramble across the gymnasium roof until one friend fell right through, amazingly escaping with only a broken leg in consequence, was graphically illustrated. So was the day when I myself attempted to ride bareback on an untrained pony.

The weekly letters almost took on a Dear Diary character as I confided my problems, my joys, my quarrels with my friends, and most of all my growing desire to overcome sin and live in a way that would be pleasing to God. The fact of my parents' love and concern, even though half a world lay between us, was in itself an important stabilising factor in my life. In all likelihood these were confidences that I would never have shared had they been present, but for Stanley and Norah such schoolgirl secrets were a bonus to compensate in some degree for their loss.

In reality, however, I was growing from adolescence into young womanhood hardly knowing my parents as people. I was building on memories of the past, and as the months turned to years these memories became blurred and idealised. I fantasised my parents' personalities until they became heroic figures of my imagination having few or none of the frailties common to the human race. Whilst they had been in China their environment had been one that I myself had shared as a small child and one with which I was familiar.

Stanley at work in Malaysia

Now I found it hard to visualise the steamy heat of the Malaysian jungles and the resettlement villages with many homes built on stilts where my parents worked.

As I completed my fifth form studies, long postal discussions took place between my parents and me regarding the future. Miss Swain was anxious for her pupil to study for a degree in English, but there were serious problems in the way of such a course, not least the fact that my educational grant expired half way through my sixth form studies, and apparently the local Welsh authority that had provided it was not prepared to extend it. The only answer appeared to be to leave school and begin a teacher training course, open at that time even to young people who had not gained any subjects at A Level. I duly applied to Stockwell College in Bromley, Kent, and was accepted to start in October 1955, shortly before my eighteenth birthday.

But Miss Swain was still unhappy. My progress on my A level work had been steady and satisfactory, and it seemed increasingly unfortunate to leave school without these qualifications. Then one night as I was casually enjoying a bath, there came a loud rap on the door; an urgent voice shouted that Miss Swain wished to see me immediately. Leaping out of my bath and hastily throwing on a few garments, I hurried along the corridor – that same wide corridor along which I had walked with so much trepidation those many years ago. What could be the reason for this pressing message? This time Miss Swain's face was all smiles. She had just received an unexpected gift of a sum of money and wished to use it to cover all my expenses for my second year in the sixth form. I was overwhelmed at the generosity of such a gesture – an act of kindness for which I would be forever grateful.

To add to my cup of happiness, my parents were due home during my second year in the sixth form and in time for Christmas 1955. As the date of their arrival grew ever closer, my excitement, coupled with a slight trepidation became yet stronger. What were my parents really like? I hardly knew. And would they recognise me? They had left me shortly after my fourteenth birthday and now I had turned eighteen. As my excitement mounted, I had a strange new perspective on my circumstances: those who had never known the pain of the long separations that missionaries' children often experienced could never know that exhilaration of anticipating the reunion. 'God more than makes up for anything we go without for his sake, doesn't he?' I wrote, but added quickly, 'I don't know that I've gone without anything except you.' It was only in later years, and with a family of my own, that I began to measure the effects of the loss of home life during the long years of my childhood, since that first separation at the age of six.

For the first few months of my parent's stay in England the mission suggested that *The Chalet* in Bidborough, currently not in use, would be a suitable home for the family. I wrote urging them to try to make alternative arrangements, for the memories attached to the house were still vivid and painful, and if to me, surely to my parents also. But in the event a joyful few weeks spent there together with Christopher went far towards baptising the home with new and happier memories.

12

AND AFTERWARDS . . .

Stanley and Norah were to be in England for eight months, and although for much of that time I was still at school studying for examinations, the sense that my parents were near at hand was a new and comforting experience. After a few weeks at The Chalet they established a temporary home in Bexley, in the south–eastern suburbs of London, not far from Chislehurst where the mission hostel was situated. There they made a home for Christopher, who had now completed his National Service and was studying at nearby Dartford College.

At last the time came for me to leave the sheltered school environment I had grown to love and to face life in the harsher community of the world outside Clarendon's peaceful grounds. The summer weeks were spent in Whitstable where Norah's eighty–one year old mother lived alone. Her father had died when Norah was still in China. Stanley's mother lived on, however, bedridden and in a nursing home.

Time passed quickly, and I was particularly grateful for the support of my parents as I tried to cope with the death of one of my closest school friends in a drowning accident. Shirley had agreed to take my place as a leader at a Christian holiday

At Whitstable with a young cousin, Summer 1956

camp in Pembrokeshire, because I wanted to spend as much time as possible with my parents. While the campers were swimming, a shifting sandbank had suddenly thrown many children out of their depth and, as Shirley tried to bring them safely to shore, she herself had been flung against a rock and concussed. Not until all the children were safe did anyone realise that Shirley was missing. The loss of my friend grieved me deeply, particularly as Shirley had taken my place at the camp. This came as a second painful reminder of the suddenness with which the lives of even young people can be cut off.

As summer turned to autumn I began to prepare to take up my place on the teacher training course at Stockwell College in Bromley, postponed for a year while I took my A Level examinations. My mother helped me to buy new clothes in preparation for this fresh experience, but now there loomed ahead yet another long separation. Before the college term began, my parents were due to sail once more for Malaysia.

Again there would be the wrench of separation, not much easier even though I was older: a separation which seemed endless as it stretched out before me, lasting, as I well knew, for a further four years.

Nor was my first year at Teacher Training College, mixing with my peers from backgrounds far different from my own, an easy or happy experience. My unsettled childhood, sheltered school environment and now the loss of any stable home base (for at nearly nineteen I was too old to return to the children's hostel in Chislehurst), ill-prepared me for the cold realities of the adult world, or for the cut and thrust of student life.

But God had not overlooked such a predicament. Throughout my school days I had been shown much kindness often from unexpected sources. And now once more timely help was provided in a way that none could have anticipated. A Christian couple, Michael and Betty Wheen, heard in a circuitous way of the need of a missionary's daughter for a home during the college vacations. Theirs was a beautiful house, spacious and comfortable, set amid extensive woodlands and situated about five miles from Stockwell College where I was training. But with five children of their own, with ages ranging from five to sixteen, they could easily have felt that they were not in a position to help. Instead they made a generous offer to accept this unknown girl into their home, not as a lodger but as one of their own daughters. Betty gave me the best bedroom in the house, insisting that I must feel able to come and go whenever I wished. This unexpected and generous provision opened up for me another home, another shelter. It brought into the vacuum of my life the sort of care and love I most needed. Practical and efficient, Betty provided me with the experience of a family–based household for the first time in my life. I began to learn how an average English household is run, how to cook, how to shop – all new things for me. The friendship and acceptance offered by the children of the family brought an important and much needed dimension to my life. My second year at college saw a much more stable and secure young woman.

After I had begun my first teaching job, this home continued to be a base during the school holidays; Christopher too was welcomed when he was in the area. His first plan after gaining his A-level grades was to continue at Dartford College with a view to studying for medicine. This did not materialise, however, for on a visit to Dublin a lively and gifted young Irish woman gained his heart. His marriage to Lillian went a long way towards eradicating hurtful memories of the past, and together he and Lillian would undertake a fruitful service for God.

I too had been giving serious thought to the future and, not unnaturally, for some time my mind had been turning towards missionary service. But any such plans were sharply curtailed when a young theological student, in a proposal swift and unexpected, asked me to marry him. Without a trace of merriment, Paul told the girl whose hand he sought that if she married him she could expect to have butter with her bread, or jam with her bread, but not bread, butter and jam. I understood the coded message instantly, and the logic appealed to me. This had been my life experience up to that very time. All my basic needs had been met in the providence of God, but I had also come to realise that God does not promise his people the luxuries of life – although he may indeed give them. I had learned too that I could serve God not just in the far–flung places of the earth but also as a

Michael takes a wedding photograph

Christian wife, and before long I accepted Paul's proposal.

Michael and Betty Wheen arranged a magnificent wedding reception for Paul and me, hiring a marquee in their woodland garden to accommodate the guests. Their own two elder daughters were to be bridesmaids, with my youngest cousin making a third. We had delayed the wedding day until after my parents arrived home from Malaysia after their four–year term of service. Just three weeks before the occasion, they were able to meet the young man to whom their daughter had given her hand and heart, and later to share in the happiness of that day.

The future did not promise to be easy. Paul's first assignment in the Christian ministry was in a town in the north of England, a place where he had already been working for almost a year while we waited my parents' return. A hard

Just married, April 1961

town spiritually, it was proving all but impervious to the
message of the Christian gospel that Paul had come to
preach. Nor was my lack of any settled family background an
easy beginning for us as a newly-married couple. But now, at
twenty-three years of age, I would experience settled home
life for the first time. And later, with the birth of our
children, would learn all the joys and perplexities that
motherhood brings to a young woman.

It had indeed been a troubled journey for both my brother and me, but as I look back over the path I have travelled, I can now see that despite the undoubted sufferings through which we had both passed – unnecessary sufferings in many respects – God has supported, protected and added unexpected provisions for our needs along the way. Even the sufferings themselves have proved to be part of God's design for my life.

After my parents officially retired from missionary work in 1976, the needs of Chinese people in the UK still occupied much of their time and concern. A Chinese Church came into being in Leicester where they were living, largely as a result of their labours. Not surprisingly, the Chinese community in that city took the veteran missionary couple to their hearts, repaying their labours with typical Chinese kindness and honour.

Several years after his return to England, my father,[1] now seventy-four years of age and still actively promoting the cause of evangelism among Chinese people, wrote to me at a time when Paul and I were facing some difficulty in the Christian work to which we were committed. He was on deputation work in Amsterdam and had been reflecting, possibly with some regrets, on the circumstances of his children's early lives. It is a letter that I will always treasure, a letter that has grown tatty and worn with re–reading:

I guess you feel life has been pretty tough on missionaries' children. It has, and on missionary parents

[1] My father died in 1988. At least fifty Chinese friends attended his funeral. My mother lived on until the age of ninety-five, first at Pilgrim Homes and then cared for by the dedicated staff of Melbourne Home, Leicester.

too, but their children didn't choose the sort of life they had to live and their parents did. I'll never forget your poor tear–stained face as we said good bye to you on your way back to school. I remember going back to our empty room fiddling about tidying the room with a heart as heavy as lead . . . There was nothing we could do about it. We had already lost our little Godfrey. You were too young to feel that much . . . We can only say that we know that suffering, for the Christian, is not the terrible thing the world thinks it to be. I don't mean we don't feel it as badly. What I do mean is we know it comes to us from our Father's loving hand and somehow he has purposes of love in permitting it. And I'm sure that is true of the things you find difficult and still do.

Such a letter went a long way towards healing the hurts of the past and helping me to see that even in the most grievous situations there is a divine purpose – a purpose still being worked out from day to day. As I look back, I can echo the words of an old hymn–writer who spoke of God's providence and care:

> My every need he richly will supply,
> Nor will his mercy ever let me die;
> In him there dwells a treasure all–divine,
> And matchless grace has made that treasure mine.

BIBLIOGRAPHY

Gordon Martin, *Chefoo School, 1881–1951*, Merlin Books Ltd., 1990.

Sheila Miller, *Pigtails, Petticoats and the Old School Tie*, OMF Publishing, 1981.

Betty Vander Els, *The Bombers' Moon*, Collins Publishers, Toronto, 1985 (a children's story written by a former pupil of the Chefoo School, and based on the same circumstances as the account in *Troubled Journey*).

ADDITIONAL BACKGROUND READING

A. J. Broomhall, *Hudson Taylor and China's Open Century*, Book 7, Hodder & Stoughton and OMF, 1989.

Norman H. Cliff, *Fierce the Conflict*, Joshua Press, 2001.

Martin Gilbert, *A History of the Twentieth Century, Volume 2, 1933–1951*, HarperCollins Publishers, 1998.

Tony Lambert, *The Resurrection of the Chinese Church*, Hodder & Stoughton and OMF Publishing, 1991.

Tony Lambert, *China's Christian Millions, The Costly Revival*, OMF Publishing, 1999.

Leslie T. Lyall, *A Passion for the Impossible, The China Inland Mission 1865–1965*, Hodder & Stoughton, 1965.

Helen Foster Snow, *My China Years*, Harrap, London, 1984.

Dr and Mrs Howard Taylor, *Hudson Taylor in Early Years*; and *Hudson Taylor and the China Inland Mission*, CIM, 1958.